NEW DIRECTIONS FOR TEACHING AND LEARNING

Marilla D. Svinicki, *University of Texas, Austin*
ASSOCIATE EDITOR

Promoting Civility: A Teaching Challenge

Steven M. Richardson
Bowling Green State University

EDITOR

Number 77, Spring 1999

JOSSEY-BASS PUBLISHERS
San Francisco

PROMOTING CIVILITY: A TEACHING CHALLENGE
Steven M. Richardson (ed.)
New Directions for Teaching and Learning, no. 77
Marilla D. Svinicki, Associate Editor

Microfilm copies of issues and articles are available in 16mm and 35mm, as well as microfiche in 105mm, through University Microfilms Inc., 300 North Zeeb Road, Ann Arbor, Michigan 48106-1346.

ISSN 0271-0633   ISBN 0-7879-4277-4

NEW DIRECTIONS FOR TEACHING AND LEARNING is part of The Jossey-Bass Higher and Adult Education Series and is published quarterly by Jossey-Bass Inc., Publishers, 350 Sansome Street, San Francisco, California 94104-1342. Periodicals postage paid at San Francisco, California, and at additional mailing offices. Postmaster: Send address changes to New Directions for Teaching and Learning, Jossey-Bass Inc., Publishers, 350 Sansome Street, San Francisco, California 94104-1342.

New Directions for Teaching and Learning is indexed in College Student Personnel Abstracts, Contents Pages in Education, and Current Index to Journals in Education (ERIC).

SUBSCRIPTIONS cost $56.00 for individuals and $99.00 for institutions, agencies, and libraries. Prices subject to change.

EDITORIAL CORRESPONDENCE should be sent to the associate editor, Marilla D. Svinicki, The Center for Teaching Effectiveness, University of Texas at Austin, Main Building 2200, Austin, TX 78712-1111.

Cover photograph by Richard Blair/Color & Light © 1990.

www.josseybass.com

CONTENTS

FROM THE SERIES EDITOR

About This Publication. Since 1980, *New Directions for Teaching and Learning* has brought a unique blend of theory, research, and practice to leaders in postsecondary education. We strive not only for solid substance but also for timeliness, compactness, and accessibility.

Our series has the following goals:

1. To inform about current and future directions in teaching and learning in postsecondary education.
2. To illuminate the context that shapes those new directions.
3. To illustrate new directions through examples from real settings.
4. To propose how new directions can be incorporated into still other settings.

This publication reflects our view that teaching deserves respect as a high form of scholarship. We believe that significant scholarship is done not only by the researcher who reports results of empirical investigations but also by the practitioner who shares with others disciplined reflections about teaching. Contributors to NDTL approach questions of teaching and learning as seriously as they approach substantive questions in their own disciplines, dealing not only with pedagogical issues but also with the intellectual and social context out of which those issues arise. Authors deal with theory and research and with practice, and they translate from research and theory to practice and back again.

About This Volume. There has been much discussion lately about the decline of civility in society and the reflection of that decline in the college classroom. Students engage in behaviors that faculty find rude, if not downright combative. Faculty engage in battles with one another over seemingly trivial matters. Yet each side bemoans the lack of civility of everyone else. This volume provides both a theoretical analysis of the problem and some very pragmatic ideas to resolve disputes and prevent them from arising in the first place.

MARILLA D. SVINICKI, associate editor, is director, Center for Teaching Effectiveness, at the University of Texas, Austin.

EDITOR'S NOTES

This volume of *New Directions for Teaching and Learning* was conceived with a focus on incivility in the classroom. In fact, when the chapter authors set up a listserv to communicate with each other, we began jokingly referring to ourselves as the "unpleasant people" in reference to the list's *unpleasantness@* address. It did not take long, however, before we realized that the joke was a depressing commentary on higher education and that we were misrepresenting the challenge that faces college teachers today. Despite well-publicized incidents of classroom violence and despite teachers' common observation that rudeness and inappropriate behavior are on the rise, serious unpleasantness is not yet the norm on most campuses. Rather than placing the greatest emphasis on dealing with such incivility, however, we have concluded that the primary challenge for teachers is to use the classroom as a place to learn acceptable behavior. To borrow a metaphor from medicine, we prefer to stress the importance of wellness instead of suggesting that teachers should specialize in triage. Hence, the title *Promoting Civility*.

Of course, incivility does happen despite our best efforts. Violence and verbal abuse are not common in most classrooms, but it is important to know what you can do if they happen in *your* classroom. At the other end of the spectrum, random acts of passive rudeness—a late arrival to class, for example, or a rustling newspaper—plague almost all college teachers. Perhaps it is easiest to grit our teeth and ignore them, but these small incivilities disturb us and other students. If teachers pretend that these incivilities do not exist, they lose opportunities to teach acceptable behavior and risk a gradual escalation of unpleasantness.

As this volume began to take form, we asked ourselves what approaches a teacher might use for encouraging appropriate behavior and anticipating occasional lapses. How might teachers manage the risks that are always present in a classroom? How can teachers make civility part of the daily lesson, and how can teachers and students learn to restore civility when it has been fractured? The result of our labors has been this volume of chapters with a constructive outlook, even when we address the topic of unpleasantness that drew us together initially.

We hope that by offering our interrelated perspectives, we have made the teacher's challenge a little less daunting. Most of all, we hope that these chapters will have injected a strain of optimism into the monotonously gloomy conversations that take place among teachers whenever student behavior falls short of our expectations. Civility can be learned.

Steven M. Richardson
Editor

STEVEN M. RICHARDSON is vice provost for undergraduate affairs and dean of under-graduate studies at Bowling Green State University.

The normal conflicts that arise within teacher-learner interaction rarely cause open incivility, but they can generate powerful emotional tensions that can destroy the relationship if they are not detected and remedied early.

Incivility in Dyadic Teaching and Learning

Richard G. Tiberius, Edred Flak

Incivility is speech or action that is disrespectful or rude. Incivility in the contemporary classroom may include insulting and even violent behavior. In the one-to-one teaching and learning situation, by contrast, such extreme forms of incivility are rarely manifested. To the casual observer even dysfunctional dyads may appear pleasant. Typically the teacher and learner smile, laugh, and converse politely. The teacher does not have to contend with disruptive outbursts from the back of the room or dominant speakers who are threatening to take over the group. In this chapter we argue that the overt civility of dyadic relationships can mask unexpressed tensions and that these tensions, if not addressed, can increase to the explosive point, at which the relationship itself is destroyed. We will use catastrophe theory—a theory formulated to explain how continuous forces can produce sudden discontinuous effects—to explain the explosive outcome of dysfunctional dyadic relationships. And we will appeal to negotiation theory and the dialectical process to build and to repair relationships.

Incivility in the dyad can be viewed as a form of communication. What it communicates is that something is wrong with the relationship that must be addressed. In classroom teaching incivility frequently is driven by other motivations. Students act out their various personal needs in classrooms with relative impunity because of their anonymity. Richard Mann (McKeachie, 1994) has described eight clusters of students—the show-off, the flatterer, the sniper, and others—who disrupt the class in various ways at the expense of the teacher. In the dyadic teaching relationship, however, there is no group protection and no third party to entertain. Consequently students are unlikely to use the dyad as a release. Incivility in the dyad is much more likely to result from negative emotions about the relationship.

Moreover, in the dyad, the expression of incivility is unlikely to be overt. It rarely manifests itself as an "event" that must be "handled" in the same sense that rude outbursts must be handled in a lecture to preserve the classroom climate. Face-to-face communication is controlled by strong norms that discourage incivility. These are motivated by fear that the relationship will worsen and that the teacher, in a position of power, might retaliate. Incivility in the dyad is often covert, commonly taking the form of silent withdrawal, uncooperativeness, or anger that threatens the quality of the teacher-learner relationship. Even more commonly, incivility in the dyad is displaced, the unexpressed negative emotions making themselves felt on written evaluations of teachers or in conversation with a fellow student, with the presiding administrator, or with the ombudsperson.

We are referring to normal conflicts and tensions that all of us have encountered in the forming of interpersonal relationships. As we come to know another person, we fit our perceptions of him or her into schemata that we have developed out of our experience with others. Our choice of schema is partly determined by our needs. If we have a need for a nurturant teacher, for example, we might tend to concentrate on the nurturant aspects of our teacher. In a sense, we do not see others as they are but as we would like them to be. If their behavior continually varies from our ideal of them and if we perceive this discrepancy, eventually we will suffer a kind of cognitive conflict or tension that we might experience as "disappointment."

The need for mutual accommodation and understanding is especially important in teacher and learner relationships. Teachers and learners must know one another if they are to facilitate learning. Teachers must understand the learners so that teachers can tailor their explanations of subject matter to the level of knowledge of the learner, or select examples that are relevant to the experience of the learner, or provide relevant feedback to the learner. Learners need to learn about their teachers too, to feel comfortable learning from them and to gain respect for them as role models.

Although the teacher may do the utmost to understand the student's needs and to provide what is needed for an optimal outcome, the best of intentions and the best skill will not result in a perfect outcome. Each of us lives a private life within our consciousness, unknown to those around us except insofar as we reveal what we experience through words, emotional display, or action. This private world is imperfectly conveyed to those around us, and their knowledge of us is therefore always incomplete and imperfect. This is a fact of the human condition. All of our relationships contain some inherent disappointment. To some extent, teachers and learners will always experience some negative feelings (pain, hurt, disappointment) in their relationships. It should be added that we are looking at the negative side of relationships. Under the best circumstances, minor negative emotions will be overshadowed by the positive feelings of excitement of learning, satisfaction of mastery, and gratitude for the gift of teaching.

Minor disappointments are more easily overcome than major ones. Although there is no way to eliminate tension and conflict from dyadic interaction, catastrophe can be prevented by dealing with the issues as they arise, thereby preventing the excessive buildup of tensions before they destroy the relationship. Indeed, conflict can even strengthen the relationship. Teachers can change their schemata or their images of their learners and vice versa by a process of mutual accommodation (Piaget, 1954). The two can come to know one another more intimately. The key to successful mutual accommodation is to structure a relationship that can handle conflicts and tensions routinely, thus preventing escalation.

The concept of relationship has both cognitive-emotional and behavioral aspects (Duck and Gilmour, 1981). The cognitive-emotional aspect acts as a set of selective filters shaping the patterns of interaction that are possible. On the cognitive-emotional side, there are certain kinds of knowledge and attitudes that can be helpful in creating a resilient teacher-learner relationship. On the behavioral side, there are certain processes, types of interaction, that facilitate mutual accommodation. Below we briefly summarize a number of recommendations for prevention and repair in teacher-learner dyads in the cognitive and emotional realm (adapted from Teitelbaum, 1990; Greben, 1985; Tiberius and Billson, 1991; and Nigam, Cameron, and Leverette, 1997). Then we make recommendations in the behavioral realm.

Cognitive and Affective Prerequisites of the Teacher-Learner Alliance

Occasional interpersonal conflict may be a normal part of human relations, but catastrophe need not be. There are ways of viewing relationships and attitudes toward one another that can help teachers and students build effective, satisfying relationships.

The Teacher-Learner Alliance: Understanding Its Importance. The first step in building resilient relationships is understanding and recognizing the importance of a teacher-learner alliance. The alliance is a partnership that is free of a disruptive level of anxiety and devoted to the learning and growth of the student (Teitelbaum, 1990). The key features of such an alliance are mutual respect and commitment to goals, shared responsibility for learning, effective communication, willingness to negotiate and understand one another, and a sense of security within the process (Tiberius and Billson, 1991). Tiberius and Billson (1991) reviewed six major research and conceptual approaches to education and concluded that the concept of the teacher-learner alliance is central to all of them. Faculty should recognize that an alliance between student and teacher early in the relationship reduces disruptive interference and enhances learning.

Accepting Disappointments and Conflicts in the Relationship as Natural Developments. If conflicts are viewed as a normal part of human relationships, they can be used positively to strengthen the relationship. Teachers are often shocked to find out that their students feel angry, withdrawn, or hurt: "What did I do to deserve this?" The point is not what a teacher did but what students perceived and how they interpreted their perceptions. Teachers need to be aware that students who interpret their actions as disrespectful may react with anger. Students who interpret their actions as lacking understanding may react with distrust and withdrawal. Students who interpret their teachers as unfair may react with anger and resentment. And students who interpret their teachers as lacking caring may react with hurt, disappointment, and anger.

Humility: Acknowledging One's Own Defensiveness, Blind Spots, and Insensitivity. Teachers must resist viewing all problems as student problems. Teachers are imperfect human beings too. Acknowledging this possibility that they may have insensitivities and blind spots is a necessary prerequisite to sharing the responsibility for relational problems. For example, one of the most common insensitivities of teachers is failure to appreciate the courage that it takes to be a learner. Learning requires a kind of humility that acknowledges ignorance. The humility is deepened when the student learns with the help of a teacher because the student has to acknowledge the superior knowledge and skill of the teacher. Students are therefore exquisitely vulnerable to criticism and ridicule. The sensitive teacher respects the courage that is required by the student in the act of learning (Svinicki, 1989). The teacher should avoid criticism and ridicule, and instead should encourage the student to learn by praising the student's willingness to tackle areas of ignorance or ineptitude as challenges that offer the opportunity for growth.

Accepting Differences of Opinion Between Teacher and Learner. Teacher and learner are not equally expert with regard to the subject matter. The teacher is expected to have more expertise. The teacher's superior understanding of the subject contributes to his or her ability to facilitate learning. Because the teacher can see the subject from many more perspectives than the learner can, the teacher can understand the learner's view and guide the learner to broaden his or her view of the subject. But the superiority of the teacher in the subject matter should not translate into thinking that the student has nothing to contribute to the understanding of the subject. Ideally, for both moral and pedagogical reasons, teachers and learners should learn from one another during their teaching-learning interaction (Freire, 1972). Even students who hold superficial and erroneous viewpoints of the subject matter are worth listening to by their teachers. They can provide teachers with valuable information about the obstacles that the teacher must overcome in helping the learner. Moreover, teachers do not have absolute knowledge of their subjects. And even if they once did, information is growing rapidly. Teachers can and should learn from their students.

Behavioral Aspects of the Teacher-Learner Alliance: Building and Repairing the Relationship Through Negotiation

Insofar as relationship problems are characterized by interpersonal conflict, the process of negotiation, which was constructed to address interpersonal conflict, should be useful in addressing them. The process of negotiation extends easily to the building and repair of relationships. The process we describe is based on the works of Fisher and Ury (1991) and Rusk (1993), although it conforms to many other writings on negotiation and effective communication (for example, Wilmot, 1979). Richardson (Chapter Eight, this volume) discusses negotiation theory in the context of leadership in academic settings. The basic process is dialectic: listen to the other's view, communicate your view to the other, and then work together to find the synthesis between your conflicting views. We describe the process in seven steps to confer more emphasis on important subprocesses.

Step One: Early Detection. The first step in preventing an explosive situation in the dyadic relationship is early detection. Each of the partners needs to be sensitive to the subtle signs of tension and dysfunction such as worrying about their relationship outside of the teaching setting, irritability, insomnia, headaches, loss of motivation, and physical upset.

Step Two: Arranging a Mutually Agreeable Time to Meet. Discussion of relationship issues takes time and should not be squeezed between pressing obligations while both partners are standing in the corridor. Moreover, both partners ought to agree on the place and time since negotiating the time and place shows respect for one another.

Step Three: Listening. It is important to establish the immediate goal as mutual understanding, not problem solving. The goal is to understand the thoughts, expectations, and feelings of the learner with regard to the issue. Listening means actively pursuing the student's central concerns, both cognitive and emotional. Listening means allowing students to tell more than the facts. The teacher should be willing to listen to the context of their situation as well as their story.

Listening techniques help the teacher hear the learner's entire message. The most obvious listening technique is a passive one: giving the learner time to talk. Teachers are accustomed to telling or explaining as their primary method of helping. Sometimes they need to be reminded that silence is necessary for some learners to speak. Other learners may benefit from a few encouraging acknowledgments such as a nod or "I see" or open-ended inquiries such as, "Could you explain?"

Active listening techniques, such as paraphrasing and affect checking, are more interactive. Paraphrasing is a brief restatement of what one partner heard the other say, in his or her own words, to give the other an opportunity to hear how the message was received and to correct it if necessary. When paraphrasing is done incessantly and obviously, though, it becomes the familiar cliché of psychobabble, the tiresome phrase: "What I'm hearing you say is . . . ." But it would be hasty to reject this useful tool just because it has become so popular. Its proper use is in dealing with emotionally charged discourse where words can be easily distorted. You might preface your paraphrase with a statement such as the following: "I would like to be certain of what you are telling me. Let me try to summarize it in my own words. Tell me if I understand it correctly or not." Paraphrase again, after making the corrections, and then ask again whether you have understood.

Affect checks are similar to paraphrases but focus on understanding the emotional content of a message—for example: "The way you phrased the problem, I'm getting the impression that you are angry that I have not been more available and you are upset about the slow progress on your proposal." Upon hearing the teacher's affect check, the student may decide that the word *angry* is not right. He or she may reply, "Not exactly 'anger.' It's more like disappointment that I feel."

Step Four: Confirming and Validating the Learner's Statement of the Problem. Paraphrasing serves only to convince the student that the teacher has understood. The teacher has not indicated what he or she thinks of the student's point of view. The learner would like to know if the teacher has dismissed it as complete rubbish or has accepted it as reasonable. The teacher needs to validate the student's statement of the problem and indicate a willingness to examine the problem as one owned by both teacher and student. The teacher is telling the student that his or her viewpoint is legitimate, valid, okay, even though it may differ from the teacher's view. The teacher might say, "I can understand why you feel disappointed. I would be disappointed too if my project was delayed because someone else was unable to meet with me."

Step Five: Expressing Empathy for the Learner. Just as the validation process communicates to students that the teacher has not only understood but appreciates the validity of their point of view, empathic expression communicates to students that the teacher appreciates the students' emotional message. Accepting the underlying hurt must be done without attacking the student. And the teacher must hold in any hurt or angry feelings. The teacher might say, "I appreciate that this must be particularly difficult for you because you are usually ahead of time in submitting your assignments and prepared way in advance for your presentations. I guess this doesn't fit with your image of yourself. If it were within your control, you would be much further ahead."

Step Six: Explaining One's Viewpoint to the Other. The ground rules of the process and the strong norm of reciprocity in dyads should provide both partners with the right to have a turn. Each should explain his or her thoughts, expectations, and feelings about the issue without blaming the other. Each should use the pronoun *I* instead of *you*: "I feel rejected" rather than "You make me feel rejected." It is sometimes difficult for teachers who are accustomed to explaining "the facts" or "truths" of their discipline to make it clear that they are expressing only their point of view, but it is important to do so. Each partner has to leave room for the other point of view. Ask for the learner to paraphrase what he or she heard you say and correct misunderstandings. It is important to remember that one's actions do not translate directly into predictable results in the other. For example, when you sit on a bench in the park, the physical response of the bench is much more predictable than is the psychological response of a person already sitting there. An engineer could predict the flex of the bench with certainty, based on a knowledge of your weight and the characteristics of the bench. In contrast, the seated person's response will depend on your actions (what you are wearing, the speed of your approach, and your facial expression). In addition, the temperament and history of the other person will affect how that person understands and responds to your approach. A person who had once been violently accosted by a stranger might feel fear, while another person might anticipate a conversation.

Step Seven: Generating Solutions. Ideally the teacher and learner should brainstorm a number of possible solutions. Brainstorming does not mean simply talking. It should be taken seriously as a communication tool. It is important that both follow the ground rules for brainstorming: write down the ideas as rapidly as they are spoken, allow no criticism until later, encourage outlandish ideas, and permit improvements on the other person's idea. Later the teacher and learner can pick through the ideas to see if any of them can form the basis of a resolution. If both are deadlocked, the partners could decide to take turns between two alternative solutions; agree to neutral arbitration, mediation, or counseling; or simply take time out to reconsider and reconvene later (Rusk, 1993). Alternatively it may be possible to agree to disagree and leave this particular issue unresolved. At least both will have gained a better understanding of the context of their disagreement and will be less likely to escalate the issue into a rejection of the entire relationship. Finally, one or the other may decide to yield (this time).

The Outcome: A Strong Teacher-Learner Alliance

The result of the process of relationship building, both cognitive-affective and behavioral, is the formation of a strong teacher-learner alliance. One element of this alliance is an agreement regarding mutual expectations and objectives. Educators refer to this agreement as an educational contract. The agreement must reconcile several disparate factors: the objectives of the educational program, the teacher's goals, the learner's goals, and both the learner's and teacher's current strengths and weaknesses. Teachers are expected to communicate their own ideas or theories, but they must also present the ideas and theories of others. Difficulties arise when the teacher fails to attend to the learner's interests and knowledge or when the learner fails to accept the teacher's strengths and limitations.

The educational contract, which clarifies the teacher's and learner's obligations to one another, focuses on the interactions between teacher and learner. The alliance includes more than an agreement about interactions. Another element of the teacher-learner alliance is the establishment of ground rules, limits, and expectations that predispose the partners toward one form of interaction or another. For example, the partners may agree about the manner and degree to which they will express personal concerns within the relationship and how these concerns will be handled. The partners reach a mutual commitment to fairness, understanding, respect, and caring (Rusk, 1993). And each of the pair demonstrates a willingness to change himself or herself to improve the relationship. Frequently, however, people are too vulnerable to handle frank, negative perceptions of themselves within a close working relationship, especially at an early stage in the development of the relationship. It is perhaps best to wait until a comfortable level of trust has developed before approaching personal topics.

Moreover, disclosures can become too intimate and frequent, thus pushing the relationship from a teacher-learner relationship to a therapeutic one. Teachers must respect the boundaries that separate the teaching role from a therapeutic one. Joseph Lowman (1984) advocates supporting students who express personal problems that interfere with their learning, but he has a rule of thumb limiting such discussions: after the student has raised such personal problems on two separate occasions, Lowman recommends advising the student to seek counseling. This rule of thumb is clearly intended to distinguish the teacher-learner relationship from a therapeutic one. Brooke (Chapter Three, this volume) makes a similar observation about dealing with students' personal disclosures about sensitive issues in the classroom.

Dealing with Trauma

When the normal process of mutual accommodation is blocked in the teacher-learner dyad, tension escalates. When the emotions become too great to contain, the relationship suddenly blows up. This rapid destruction of the relationship can be viewed as an interpersonal catastrophe, using *catastrophe* in the technical sense as the discontinuous event resulting from underlying continuous variables when their limits have been exceeded (Zeeman, 1977). After catastrophe has occurred, the two are likely to be emotionally traumatized. This makes it more difficult to apply the skill of negotiation. They will need to cool down, or the teacher-learner alliance may be destroyed.

After the teacher-learner relationship has suffered a trauma, the relationship assumes an adversarial character in which the two have too little trust to enter into effective negotiation. Each may dig in to a hardened position and demand concessions of the other. Or, even more likely, they will attempt to leave the relationship. Because they are so invested in the success of the relationship (see Palmer, 1998), the work of repairing the damage to their relationship may be painful and difficult. Neither party is likely to feel comfortable with the acknowledgment of failure in the relationship. Incivility on the part of the student implies that the student is blaming the teacher; the uncivil action constitutes an indictment of the teacher and a disavowal on the part of the student for responsibility for the breakdown. This can be extremely painful for the teacher, especially one who has invested sincerely in trying to connect meaningfully with the student. The teacher's dismay at this point constitutes a major obstacle to focusing attention on the task of repair rather than on the task of preserving self-esteem.

In the face of such open incivility, a major temptation for the teacher is to retaliate against the criticism by taking the offensive, criticizing, or even dismissing the student. Even our characterization of the student's response as an incivility betrays a preconceived idea that the teacher is in the right and the student is in the wrong, if only for having behaved so badly. Taking the one-up position is not very useful, however, and the student may interpret it as sanctimonious posturing. Under such extreme conditions we recommend a process of trauma repair, which requires the creation of a safe environment, an exploration of the trauma, and an integration of the new knowledge (Herman, 1992).

Creating a Safe Environment. Creating a safe environment is the prerequisite for any progress. A constructive, climate-setting conversation can open in many ways. One way is to begin by exchanging expressions of positive intention. It is comforting to know that each is willing to try. Another is to try to reduce power imbalances by taking a one-down position or a neutral position. If there is the luxury of time, the teacher and learner can take some time out or consult a third party, a counselor, or a neutral facilitator.

Exploring the Trauma. The unwanted behavior—fear, negativism, blocking—that accompanies trauma results from a sequence of mental events. The sequence moves from perception to cognition to emotion and results in behavior. Once the partners feel safe, they can begin to analyze the elements of the sequence one at a time. The analysis can employ the processes of active listening described above: using paraphrasing and validation to explore discrepancies in one another's perceptions and cognitions and using affect checks and empathy to explore discrepancies in one another's emotions. The difference between the use of these procedures in trauma reduction and their use in everyday relationship building is a matter of time and concentration; much more of both are devoted to trauma repair.

Integrating the New Knowledge. Finally the partners can attempt to integrate what they have learned into their relationship. If the process of repair has gone well, the relationship can not only be repaired but also strengthened by this process. A new relationship emerges.

Conclusion

We have used the words *catastrophe* and *trauma* in their theoretical senses throughout this chapter. We recognize that in the context of educational practice, these words are emotionally loaded. Ordinarily authors should offer an apology for emotionally loaded words in scholarly work. However, it occurs to us that the emotional connotations of these terms are appropriate in this context. We recall colleagues, in the setting of our medical school, who have received highly critical comments about their relationships with residents after teaching them in one-to-one situations over periods of six months to a year, with not a single clue that anything was wrong. The effect of this feedback has been extremely dispiriting to the teachers. Anger, discouragement, and frustration were common reactions. One teacher said he felt betrayed. Another perhaps epitomized the feeling behind their reactions: "I can't believe it. I have been working closely with these residents for two years. Their faces pass through my mind, and I wonder which one of them would stab me in the back. I liked them all, and they all seemed to like me." Our writing has been motivated partly out of the desire to help these teachers.

References

Duck, S., and Gilmour, R. *Personal Relationships I: Studying Personal Relationships.* Orlando, Fla.: Academic Press, 1981.

Fisher, R., and Ury, W. *Getting to Yes: Negotiating Agreement Without Giving In.* (2nd ed.) New York: Penguin, 1991.

Freire, P. *Pedagogy of the Oppressed.* New York: Herder and Herder, 1972.

Greben, S. E. "Dear Brutus: Dealing with Unresponsiveness Through Supervision." *Canadian Journal of Psychiatry,* 1985, *30,* 48–53.

Herman, J. L. *Trauma and Recovery.* New York: Basic Books, 1992.

Lowman, J. *Mastering the Techniques of Teaching.* San Francisco: Jossey-Bass, 1984.

McKeachie, W. J. *Teaching Tips: Strategies, Research and Theory for College and University Teachers.* (9th ed.) Lexington, Mass.: Heath, 1994.

Nigam, T., Cameron, P. M., and Leverette, J. S. "Impasses in the Supervisory Process: A Resident's Perspective." *American Journal of Psychotherapy,* 1997, *51* (2), 252–273.

Palmer, P. J. *The Courage to Teach: Exploring the Inner Landscape of a Teacher's Life.* San Francisco: Jossey-Bass, 1998.

Piaget, J. *The Construction of Reality in the Child.* New York: Basic Books, 1954.

Rusk, T. *The Power of Ethical Persuasion.* New York: Viking Penguin, 1993.

Svinicki, M. "If Learning Involves Risk-Taking, Teaching Involves Trust-Building." *Teaching Excellence,* Fall 1989.

Teitelbaum, S. H. "Aspects of the Contract in Psychotherapy Supervision." *Psychoanalysis and Psychotherapy,* 1990, *8,* 95–98.

Tiberius, R. G., and Billson, J. M. "The Social Context of Teaching and Learning." In R. J. Menges and M. D. Svinicki (eds.), *College Teaching: From Theory to Practice.* New Directions for Teaching and Learning, no. 45. San Francisco: Jossey-Bass, 1991.

Wilmot, W. W. *Dyadic Communication.* (2nd ed.) Reading, Mass.: Addison-Wesley, 1979.

Zeeman, E. C. *Catastrophe Theory.* Reading, Mass.: Addison-Wesley, 1977.

RICHARD G. TIBERIUS is professor in the Department of Psychiatry, University of Toronto, and at the Centre for Research in Education.

EDRED FLAK is associate professor in the Department of Psychiatry, University of Toronto.

How do emotions develop? In this chapter models are presented that aid in explaining the ways our assumptions affect how we react emotionally and behaviorally.

Promoting Internal Civility: Understanding Our Beliefs About Teaching and Students

Sally L. Kuhlenschmidt

A common variable in uncivil behavior is strong emotional reaction. Simple observation reveals an apparent relationship between expression of anger or frustration and inappropriate behaviors. A student is angry over a failing grade and storms out of the classroom shouting at the professor. An instructor, frustrated because students do not read the material, browbeats them for an hour. Many instructors feel anxious or upset when reflecting on personal experiences with uncivil behavior.

Emotional reactions are not, in and of themselves, the problem. Recognizing and accepting your feelings is generally necessary for overall healthy adjustment. The problem is inappropriate behavior that occurs as a consequence of strong emotions. Intense emotions increase the odds of behaving in a way that will create interpersonal and other problems. If distressing emotion could be moderated, then inappropriate behaviors might be reduced.

How Do Strong Emotions Develop?

Humans tend to attribute emotional reactions to influences from others (saying, for example, "He made me angry"). This informal theory or belief, however, falls short on several counts. It does not explain how two persons who experience an identical event could experience quite different emotions. It also offers no mechanism for transmission. Does the person who "made" you angry beam thought waves from his head to yours? Ellis and Harper (1997), in their rational emotive behavior therapy model, propose an alternative mechanism for understanding the development of emotion that can help individuals moderate or manage their own emotional reactions.

Imagine that two teachers have experienced an identical event, such as students' cheating. One declares, "That's life," and proceeds relatively calmly to address the problem. The other proclaims, "Students should not cheat! It isn't right!" and becomes outraged. The person may act on his outrage by slamming things down, waving his arms, or shouting. What makes the difference in the emotional reactions? Ellis and Harper (1997) theorized that what you say to yourself about an event (a self-statement or belief) is the determining factor in the kind and intensity of emotion that you experience. Although many people believe their emotions come first and then verbal expressions, Ellis argues that self-statements precede emotional reactions. In the example, the outraged individual judged the event ("It shouldn't happen. It isn't fair") and then reacted emotionally based on that judgment. The calm individual also made a judgment ("That's life") and reacted with milder levels of emotion.

In a classroom, you have probably seen two students receive identical grades; one responds with relief, another with dismay. You do not "cause" the students to feel as they do. Their internal messages about an event result in their emotional reactions. Similarly, when you are upset with a student for doing or not doing something, this student is not beaming thought waves into your head to cause your reaction. The student cannot "make" you angry. You make yourself angry or discouraged or elated. Your self-statements are the cause of how you react to any situation.

Ellis would argue that emotions result not from an external stimulus but an internal one. Some internal statements are more likely than others to generate strong emotion. These are statements that are literally illogical. The statements may be overgeneralizations (for example, "One student marked my ratings low. I'll never be a good teacher"), or they may be literally untrue (for example, "I must be perfect"). Statements such as, "He made me angry," are illogical because anger (or love or boredom) is internally generated from personal perceptions of events. Other people cannot make you angry. Their behavior may increase the chances of an emotional interpretation, but they cannot force the changes associated with strong emotion. One consequence of this model is that the individual is fully in control of his or her own emotional state.

There are two caveats about causality and emotion. First, some individuals are not ready to take personal responsibility for their emotional state. It is much easier to blame someone else for unhappiness. It follows that people typically do not appreciate being told bluntly, particularly in the midst of righteous anger, that they are responsible for their own emotions. Suggestions later in this chapter will describe more diplomatic ways of helping people, including yourself, ameliorate strong emotional reactions that are interfering with instruction.

The second caveat is that even if we cannot guarantee or cause feelings in another, our behavior can increase the probabilities that another person will make self-statements that lead to happiness or to upset. Predicting emotional reactions to any specific behavior is made possible only by sharing a culture. A culture has shared self-statements about what is fair and what is unjust (cultural values). If you were to visit a very different culture, you might quickly run into problems because you no longer share a set of statements with those around you. When I was teaching in a foreign country, some of my students blatantly looked at others' exams. My impression of the country's values was that the social level of the student determined whether "looking" was justified. "Looking" was not defined as cheating under certain cultural circumstances. The locals were surprised that I considered looking inappropriate across the board.

Although you do not directly cause emotional reactions in others, your behavior may influence which self-statements an individual makes. Your local culture will also place some responsibility on you for the effects of your behavior on others. To the extent that you wish to operate over the long term in a social group, then you may wish to adjust your behavior to fit local norms.

Sources of What We Tell Ourselves

Ellis said our interpretations of events are the result of assumptions learned very early in life. The assumptions are so ingrained that we are often unaware that they exist, as a fish is unaware of the water in which it lives. A common assumption is, "I should be liked by everyone." This assumption can result in passive or overly accommodating behavior, which may lead to more behavior management problems in the classroom. Close examination reveals that being liked by everyone is an illogical assumption. The vast majority of the planet's population does not know you. Of those who do know you, personality conflicts are certain to occur with a subset. Another portion of humanity is incapable of empathetic connection, much less love. Finally, it takes time and repeated contacts to develop affection, unrealistic for most of our acquaintances. A more reasonable statement would be, "I would prefer it if people liked me, but I can accept that it will not always happen."

To identify ingrained beliefs or self-statements, you may need to begin by identifying a situation in which you experience a strong emotion and work backward to identify self-statements. I had a school principal write in a paper for my class that he did not trust book learning. At first I was so outraged I felt it wisest not to grade his paper until I was calmer. As I reflected on the circumstances, I eventually identified that I had made several assumptions grounded in my identity as a scholar: "everyone should learn from books," "educational administrators should value learning from books," and, most central, "the administrator should agree with my values." Once I understood what assumptions I was making, I was able to reflect that the principal was working with students from a rural area. In such circumstances, books might not be very effective teaching tools. Another explanation could be that he had not reflected on some disadvantages of learning from life experiences. And I realized that I needed to reflect more on the disadvantages of books and the values to be obtained from experiential learning. I greatly modified my comments to offer some questions and reflective commentary rather than a condemnation.

The only absolute in life is death. Therefore, any other absolute statement (a statement using *shoulds, musts, oughts,* or variants) is not a reflection of reality. These statements are irrational or illogical. To proclaim, "I must not make mistakes," or, "Students should turn papers in on time," is to deny reality. There are consequences for making mistakes or not turning papers in on time, but those consequences may be choices for some or reflections of reality. Sometimes the *shoulds* or *oughts* come from a desire to avoid a severe (or perceived to be severe) consequence. "I must swim for shore or drown" is recognition of a narrow, unpleasant choice of options. Nevertheless, Ellis would say it is still a choice within the individual's control, not an absolute. The person could choose to drown.

Ellis does not assume that there *should* be a pleasant choice in every circumstance, nor does he assume that individuals *ought* to be happy and satisfied with available options. He acknowledges that life would be nicer if choices were pleasant, but he does not expect what cannot be. Some find this worldview very uncomfortable or frightening. A common Western assumption is that the world should be a just place (Lerner and Miller, 1978). The notion that it is not can be disturbing. On the other hand, it can also be liberating. Fears of being cheated, overlooked, or endangered can be replaced with an acknowledgment that these things may happen, but you may also get more than you deserve. You learn to enjoy what you have now. You may find that life is about the journey. You can forgive yourself and others for what fate has contributed to life.

Not all self-statements are problematic, but some are more likely than others to result in strong emotion and potentially uncivil behavior. In general, statements involving *shoulds, musts,* or *oughts* are more likely to produce intense feelings. Clark (1998), however, distinguishes between preferred and absolute statements or beliefs. Self-statements accepted as absolute or unchangeable rules, rather than preferred states of being, result in stronger feeling, and potentially more uncivil behavior. We may, however, understand that a belief ("I should not make any mistakes") is a preferred state of being rather than absolute rule. When a mistake occurs, persons who know their beliefs are preferred can accept the mistake gracefully and move on. For example, we would like to make no mistakes and we try not to make them, but we accept that mistakes will happen. Persons who think their beliefs are universal rules (absolutes) are more likely to react with great emotion. They are more rigid in their options for behavior, their emotions are more likely to be driven by events beyond their control.

Again, strong feeling in itself is not the problem. The problem arises from destructive behavior as a result of that strong emotion. Failing to recognize our strong feelings is likely to lead to other types of problems.

Challenging Irrational Beliefs

To reduce or eliminate unproductive emotional reactions, Ellis advises identifying absolute *shoulds, oughts,* and *musts* and countering them. For example, an instructor who becomes very upset with late papers could feel this way because of a self-statement such as, "Students should follow my rules." Countering statements might include, "I would prefer it if they turned papers in on time, but they are independent human beings who will make their own choices." Another possible countering statement could be, "It is easier on me and them when the rules are followed, but it is unrealistic to expect complete compliance." The exact nature of an effective countering statement depends on the individual and is best generated by the concerned party, perhaps with some assistance.

Typically there are several levels of self-statements or assumptions that would be explored for a particular circumstance. For the example about late papers, the instructor may realize with further reflection that he holds broader assumptions about authority. These more general assumptions drive his attitudes about students' following his syllabus. For example, he may believe, "Authority should be obeyed" or "I have the best interests of the students at heart; therefore they ought to do what I say." In general, it takes time to uncover the full range of self-statements that affect a particular situation. Countering statements lead to milder emotions, which result in more effective problem solving and behaviors.

When strong emotion occurs in self or others, consider what assumptions are driving that emotion. How could the situation be evaluated more realistically and accurately? The time to intervene with countering statements is as early as possible. Offering countering statements in an aggressive or intimidating manner is likely to be ineffective in most circumstances. Core assumptions are deeply held and most likely to be altered in a supportive and safe atmosphere. It is illogical, after all, to believe that people should, must, or ought to be logical in their thinking. It is also illogical to believe that a person must develop his or her rational thinking at a particular pace or to a particular depth at a time convenient for the teacher.

Ellis's theory speaks to the exceptional circumstance most effectively. This theory is most powerful when an illogical assumption or belief has distorted or interfered with the person's capacity to adapt to the world around her. In the diverse classroom, the instructor will encounter persons who do not share her beliefs and assumptions about the educational world. Some students place values on socializing or visiting with family or working instead of doing the classroom tasks. An instructor who persistently expects all students to conform to her educational assumptions about the world is in danger of disillusionment and frustration. An escalating power struggle may result in which the instructor increases demands because the students *should* conform.

The person in a position of authority (instructor, administrator, faculty development director) who is aware of this model can more readily recognize illogical thinking in others. This person can be more understanding and perhaps help others identify and counter unproductive self-statements.

The Effect of Illogical Beliefs on the Learning and Teaching Process

Each instructional decision is an expression of the instructor's belief. Some students share those beliefs and do well. Some do not and do poorly. In some sense education is the act of creating shared beliefs in those being educated. Most students arrive at college wanting to adopt those shared beliefs. Listing objectives of the course in the syllabus is a way of detailing the values and assumptions (or "oughts") that will arise from the shared educational experience. Grading is a measure of the extent to which the student has adopted the core assumptions of the discipline. Failure to meet those expectations results in a lower grade.

Student failure does not have to result in instructor guilt or anger (for example, "He ought to know better than to answer this way"). It is irrational to believe that every student must succeed, although it is useful for instructor growth, planning, and motivational purposes. Some students arrive at an educational institution not willing or ready to change or grow, despite their intentions. Imposing a time line on them is illogical. Human learning follows its own course. I might prefer it if all students learned from my experiences and interpretations, and I might keep trying to reach every student, but it is unreasonable to expect success every time. My experiences simply will not be valid for everyone.

When I acknowledge this limitation, then I can examine my approaches and increase the variety of tools and methods I use in interactions with students. I can journey with them rather than lead them, at least ideally. I can respond more realistically to their needs rather than responding to my need. We find it more *efficient* for students to conform to us. Many of our pedagogical decisions are and will always be based on the realistic need to use our limited resources effectively. It is more efficient, but it does not always produce the desired (by the student or the instructor) result in the student. Aside from these broader teaching and learning issues, illogical beliefs may have more specific implications for students as they adjust to the university, for new faculty as they adjust to the students, and for all faculty as they face the issue of improving their teaching.

Student Reactions. Students come to the education enterprise with an entire set of assumptions about the world. The academic environment is generally constructed to challenge values or beliefs in various disciplines. We like to believe that participants in the educational enterprise should learn to think critically.

Individuals have varying tolerance for being challenged, depending on their life experiences and abilities. One individual may enjoy debate and seek it; another may crumble. Ellis would likely explain this variability as due to student theories or beliefs regarding their own capacity for handling challenge. Someone who becomes hostile in a debate may assume, "The person who directly questions me is attacking me personally." Those who have a prolonged and strong reaction to corrections on papers may have a similar belief. It may be helpful for an instructor to provide some generally applicable countering arguments to students before returning marked papers. For example, the instructor may explain that it is normal to submit papers to repeated editing (rather than believe that papers ought to be created fully formed). The instructor could lead students in the class in identifying their irrational beliefs about writing.

New Faculty In my experience, new faculty commonly do not realize how unusual their own academic skills are and are surprised at the wide range of performance in their students. They may have great difficulty understanding that a student may do a mediocre or poor job for any of a variety of reasons, including choice. Faculty may take poor performance personally, believing that all students ought to strive for the faculty standards of performance or that all students should want to succeed. They may see student failure as a personal failure. Detail-driven faculty may obsess over bringing a single student up to their very high standards, much to the distress of the student, who has other life values. Until the issue is understood from the student's perspective and self-statements, interventions may be ineffective in specific cases. An instructor who takes student failure personally may publicly condemn exam performance, increasing the odds of students' feeling humiliated. If faculty understand that high standards are their own ideal, not an absolute rule of the universe, they may be more patient with students and happier when teaching. They may take the time to explain to students why high standards are important and how they will affect a student's life instead of assuming that students see the world as teachers do.

Faculty Improvement. Effective teaching skills can increase the odds of students' learning the material and adapting to the educational environment. Those skills can be learned. The faculty member wishing to improve his or her teaching abilities has a mental balancing act to perform. A desire to be successful with students is typically what drives teachers to improve their skills. What happens, however, when that desire runs into natural limits?

Laboratory data suggest several ways instructors might react to this conflict. In early learning experiments (Maier, 1949; Maier, Glazer, and Klee, 1940; Maier and Klee, 1945; Seligman and Maier, 1967) animals were required to respond in impossible situations that had no escape or correct response. They had no way to control the outcome. Depending on experimental variables, the animals developed fixated behavior (repeating the action whatever the environment), and they deteriorated physically; some became passive, waiting for events to happen to them rather than respond. Most alarming, some failed to change their behavior when the situation became solvable, that is, they lost the capacity to learn. This cluster of behaviors can be thought of as helplessness. Hiroto (1974) found similar results with humans but found that perceived control determined the outcomes. Those who believe life events are the result of chance displayed more of the helpless behaviors than those who believe their skills can influence outcomes.

Teaching presents several situations that could be interpreted as impossible. Providing what some students desire (for example, an essay exam) upsets other students (who want multiple choice). Another impossible situation is that interpretation of student ratings is inevitably somewhat judgmental, yet salary and promotion may depend on them. Some teachers, frustrated by the impossible tasks, simply repeat their patterns year in and year out. Or they are likely to believe that teaching is a talent, not a skill. Or they may declare that the latest ideology is the solution to all teaching problems and apply it whatever the situation. Some instructors may deteriorate physically, perhaps displaying depression or addictive behavior, particularly around evaluation times. They may be angry in response to student ratings precisely because they feel so helpless in the face of those ratings and administrative interpretation of them. Some instructors withdraw physically or mentally from their students. They may resist training in pedagogy. To admit they could improve their skills is to have to face the responsibility for failing with some. Any number of uncivil acts can result from these responses to a perceived impossible situation. The Ellis model might suggest that these teachers who feel out of control have developed rigid and illogical beliefs, such as, "Teaching should be done this way," or, "I shouldn't feel helpless or uncertain when teaching."

Although those who believe they can control events likely display less helplessness, they are not necessarily better off in terms of civil behavior. Their efforts at control in an impossible situation may take the form of aggression and domination. When a course is required, teacher aggression places the student in a similarly impossible situation. Students may react with repetitive or stereotyped behavior (saying, "Will this be on the exam?" or seeking "the" right answer). They may deteriorate physically. They may withdraw literally or in their behavior. Or they may become aggressive (for example, by sleeping in class). Their aggression might spark further aggression from the instructor, who is also trying to exert control. This is a model that could explain the escalation of aggression in some classes. It does not explain why it is effective to provide some structure to students who are learning, but it might be useful in certain situations. The Hiroto model suggests that giving students some choice, for example, in papers or topics covered in class, may be helpful.

Understanding why you may respond with these patterns does not necessarily make it easier to accept when it happens to you. The person who most values students and teaching may be at most risk for developing helplessness. The more important an event is to the individual, the more likely it is that difficulty in the event will result in feelings of helplessness. Repeated experience with lack-of-control situations is more likely to result in problems. My experience is that persons with high standards focus on the problem elements and not the success elements. They will target the single negative statement in a group of student comments or the lowest ratings and take the higher ones for granted. They may also overgeneralize that comment ("I am no good as a teacher, and I ought to be") rather than accurately applying it ("This one student was not satisfied. Is it reasonable for me to respond to this problem? Is it a consequence of some behavior others find satisfying?"). Always seeing the negative is putting oneself in an impossible situation.

Realistic self-evaluation is important for maintaining an effective problem-solving approach toward teaching (Franken, 1988). Faculty development directors and instructors may find it useful to provide early success experiences to their trainees. Sometimes it may be necessary to draw attention to the successes. Encouraging persons to take a longer term view of teaching and learning is more realistic, recognizing that it is a skill and an art to be developed over time. Teaching and learning skills will actually change as the nature of education alters with cultural changes.

Like the animals placed in the impossible situations, there can be a fundamental conflict between our high standards and reality. Teachers who conclude, "I cannot and never will control student outcomes and behavior though I should," have placed themselves in an impossible situation. Teachers who conclude, "I can eventually influence student outcomes and behaviors, even though I cannot be successful 100 percent of the time," have adopted an attitude that is likely to be more effective over the long term. It is the difference between striving for perfection (impossible) versus striving for excellence (possible).

Exceptions to These Models of Emotions

There are occasions when strong emotion is caused by a chemical imbalance (for example, persons with bipolar disorder or someone on drugs) or physiological problem (for example, brain damage). In such circumstances, countering statements may only confuse or irritate the person who is upset. Reasoning with a person whose faculties are disrupted by chemicals or physiology is unlikely to be effective. If you suspect the behavior is influenced by one of these factors, you may be able to help the person focus. Reduce extraneous factors (for example, by asking him to step into the hall or dismissing others). It may be necessary to send for help in dealing with this individual.

Other behaviors on your part can help to manage the person's response. Remaining calm helps cue the person to stay calm. Moving slowly and gently, yet firmly, encourages similar responses from the individual. The person experiencing one of these physical problems has impaired capacity to attend and may be receiving very distorted sensory signals. He is likely incapable of sorting out what to attend to. Any direction you can give will be important. It may be necessary to direct attention explicitly to your face, then explicitly ask him to listen a moment, then give calm direction for behavior. The simpler that direction is, the more likely he is to be able to follow it.

Conclusion

It is not wrong to make assumptions about the world. They serve many purposes, such as making life understandable or seem safe and organized. For some persons a feeling of safety is necessary before they can function, even if safety is an illusion. Assumptions are often grounded in real experiences (for example, not obeying authority often results in unpleasant consequences). Shared beliefs and assumptions help smooth social interactions among groups of similarly minded people. At a minimum, beliefs or assumptions that are totally unrealistic (for example, "The world is flat") provide some measure of comfort to the believer simply because familiarity is comfortable and change is painful.

For those willing to examine their assumptions, however, these models suggest methods for dealing with the internal and external incivilities we encounter as teachers. The models also have implications for understanding student behavior and sometimes suggest methods for dealing with student behavior. There are circumstances in which understanding does not mean successful management of behavior. Nevertheless, greater tolerance can be a useful tool in the ongoing process that is teaching and learning.

References

Clark, L. *SOS: Help for Emotions.* Bowling Green, Ky.: Parents Press, 1998.

Ellis, A., and Harper, R. *A Guide to Rational Living.* (3rd ed.) North Hollywood, Calif.: Wilshire Book Co., 1997.

Franken, R. *Human Motivation.* (2nd ed.) Pacific Grove, Calif.: Brooks/Cole, 1988.

Hiroto, D. "Locus of Control and Learned Helplessness." *Journal of Experimental Psychology,* 1974, *102,* 187–193.

Lerner, M., and Miller, D. "Just World Research and the Attribution Process: Looking Back and Ahead." *Psychological Bulletin,* 1978, *85,* 1030–1051.

Maier, N. *Frustration: The Study of Behavior Without a Goal.* New York: McGraw-Hill, 1949.

Maier, N., Glazer, N., and Klee, J. "Studies of Abnormal Behavior in the Rat: III. The Development of Behavior Fixations Through Frustration." *Journal of Experimental Psychology,* 1940, *26,* 521–546.

Maier, N., and Klee, J. "Studies of Abnormal Behavior in the Rat: XVII. Guidance Versus Trial and Error in the Alteration of Habits and Fixations." *Journal of Psychology,* 1945, *19,* 133–163.

Seligman, M., and Maier, S. "Failure to Escape Shock." *Journal of Experimental Psychology,* 1967, *74,* 1–9.

SALLY L. KUHLENSCHMIDT is director of the Center for Teaching and Learning and associate professor of psychology at Western Kentucky University in Bowling Green, Kentucky.

Sensitive issues are an inherent part of some course content. The author has learned how to negotiate sensitive topics while developing a sense of community in a large human sexuality class.

Feelings from the Back Row: Negotiating Sensitive Issues in Large Classes

Corly Petersen Brooke

Dear Dr. Brooke, I am not attending Human Sexuality class today because I do not feel up to dealing with the issue of rape at the moment. Four years ago when I was fifteen years old I was raped on Christmas Day while on vacation. Normally I do not have any trouble talking about and dealing with the issue of rape but right now I am so stressed out I am about to cry anyway, so I know I can't handle being in class today. I am sure you understand. Thank you. *(Susan, sophomore in Family Services)*

Susan—Thank you for sharing this with me. I am sorry this happened to you and I would be more than willing to talk with you about this. It's important you not keep it to yourself. Your feelings about it probably are not predictable and there is a lot of good help available. I would be happy to share with you the excellent resources I know of in our community to assist you. It takes a lot of courage to reach out. You are in my thoughts. You certainly are not alone in this. I'm here if you need to talk. *Dr. Brooke*

Seven years ago the opportunity arose for me to teach a course on human sexuality at a large, midwestern university. Because the course was offered in the College of Family and Consumer Sciences, I was eager to approach the topic of sexuality from a holistic, life-span perspective that was based on family life. I had little idea of the impact this course would have on my teaching style and my increased sensitivity to my students.

The course rapidly grew in popularity, and I soon found myself facing 325 students in a large auditorium teaching a highly sensitive and personal topic. My first challenge was to overcome my own reticence to teach such sensitive material openly. Although our society provides many venues for gratuitous and violent portrayals of sexuality, we cloak much of relevant sexuality information in secrecy, locked in a system of moral and social taboos. Granted, sexuality is a highly intimate and personal topic, yet students often engage in risk-taking behaviors without accurate knowledge (Maddock, 1997; Strong and DeVault, 1997). Although I was dedicated to maintaining the scholarly integrity of the course, I was continually aware that what I was teaching would be interpreted through a diverse range of values and moral beliefs, as well as unique personal experiences. Although the content was sensitive, I wanted to address issues that the students were personally struggling with in their daily lives. Each day as I entered the classroom, I felt I needed to balance delicately the intellectual pursuit of knowledge with sensitivity to emotional and social issues.

I decided to focus on my primary objective of optimizing the sexual health and well-being of the students while providing opportunities to keep channels of communication open by requesting and supporting individuals' efforts to understand and express their ideas, feelings, and questions. This meant that I began a journey of discovering pedagogical methods that would provide these opportunities while maintaining high scholarly standards for the course. This journey continues to teach me skills of adaptation, experimentation, flexibility, risk taking, and collaboration. In our contemporary social climate, many academic courses inherently embody delicate topics, and many educators find themselves in relatively similar situations in regard to potentially sensitive issues. I respect and appreciate differences in individual teaching styles. I recognize therefore that I have dealt with sensitive issues in ways that reflect my own style and that other teachers might handle them differently. At the risk of sounding didactic and omniscient, however, I would like to share some of the outcomes of my journey along this pedagogical path.

Sensitive Issues Statement

Coincidentally, as I began teaching the sexuality course, a highly sensitized issue became a catalyst for public debate. A sexually explicit video had been shown, unannounced, to a foreign language class at another university in the state system, and an irate parent had complained to the state board of regents. In response, the regents asked each of the three state-supported institutions to develop a policy for presenting sensitive material to students. Suddenly I found myself at the center of a raging debate in our faculty senate. I spoke passionately of the need to protect academic freedom in the classroom. I also explained that most of the material I presented in the human sexuality class was sensitive in nature and I could not possibly anticipate which topics would be sensitive for each student, thereby making any policy burdensome to execute. Nevertheless, the faculty senate passed the following policy to notify students regarding sexually explicit class content:

For sound pedagogical reasons, a faculty member may decide to use course materials that include explicit visual representations of human sexual acts. The faculty member has an obligation to inform students at the beginning of the course about the nature of that material. If a student chooses not to view the presentation(s) and the faculty member determines that alternative assignment(s) are not feasible, the student shall be permitted to drop the course without penalty (as an administrative drop) within seven calendar days of the class being so informed. [Iowa State University Faculty Senate, Sept. 7, 1993]

Although I personally objected to the policy I felt obligated to implement it. Therefore, I now include the following paragraphs on my Human Sexuality course syllabus:

Welcome to Human Sexuality! This course is designed to educate you about the important topic of human sexuality. Although this is a large lecture class format, we have worked to provide you with opportunities to individually process information and to ask questions. We believe that effective education is a two-way exchange and, therefore, we encourage you to become an active participant in this course and hope that you will gain knowledge that will enhance your decision-making throughout life. The basic ground rule for class discussion is RESPECT. We expect diversity in beliefs and values related to sexuality issues. We ask you to always maintain respect for opinions differing from your own which may be presented in class.

Sensitive Issues: Due to the inherent content of this human sexuality course, much of the material will be sexually explicit. Also lectures, assigned reading, class exercises, discussions and workbook assignments will cover sensitive issues. We will prepare you for these topics; however sensitivity is an individual matter often dependent upon unique life experiences. If you wish to discuss individual concerns please contact us during office hours or make an individual appointment.

On the first day of each semester, I discuss these two paragraphs in detail with the students. Although I disagreed with the policy initially, I have found that this practice has improved the course in two major ways. First, it creates a basis for all class discussions and questions to be conducted from a foundation of respect. I emphasize that it takes courage to speak out in a large classroom, particularly on a sensitive issue. As Tierney (1993) states, "It is a struggle to create an environment where different voices are heard and everyone is a learner" for we "open the possibility for disagreement and conflict" (pp. 153, 155). I make it clear to the students that vigorous debate within respectful boundaries can help us to understand each other's realities and differences (Tierney, 1993). However, I also clarify that I will not condone snickering, whispering, or other derogatory behaviors and that if such behaviors occur, I will address them directly. Insubordination, intimidation, and disrespect will not be tolerated in this classroom (Schneider, 1998). I encourage spontaneous questions and active participation in the class, and I feel it is important that the students understand the parameters. I have found that this has increased the frequency of questions and comments in class. I have also found that although it is difficult, I often do have to reinforce the standard of respect, which offers the opportunity to review the foundation of acceptance of differing views in the class.

The students feel passionately about many of the topics presented in class and through the assigned readings. Learning can be an emotional experience that is not necessarily joyful and can even seem distressing when change is occurring and past beliefs are challenged (Brookfield, 1990). Productive debate frequently occurs, and classroom tension can rise. Occasionally I find it is important to intervene and redirect a discussion if the emotional intensity becomes overly passionate. I do not hesitate to intervene if speech degenerates into a derogatory, personal attack. Although I want to model acceptance of diverse viewpoints, I do not want disagreements to evolve into public disputes that create a hostile win-lose environment and digress from scholarly integrity (Keltner, 1998).

Second, although I obviously cannot anticipate what is potentially sensitive for each student, I have found that announcing highly sensitive topics well ahead of time has been beneficial. I agree with Arthur Levine that "students are coming to college overwhelmed and more damaged than in the past" (Levine and Cureton, 1998, p. 15). Advance preparation for acutely sensitive topics models respects and creates appreciation for the diverse experiences of classmates. I post upcoming topics at least two weeks ahead of time on the chalkboard and discuss the potential sensitivity of the topic. I also include advance preparation for videos on such topics as birthing, sexual violence, media exploitations, and sexually transmitted diseases. Although this is obviously good methodology, the personal impact was made clear to me when I announced three weeks in advance that we would be discussing the topic of rape and would be viewing a nonexplicit video on that topic. I was contacted by two students, one of whom asked to bring her counselor with her to class for personal support and another survivor of rape who asked to bring a supportive friend with her on that day. I also received the e-mail at the beginning of this article, which caused me to adapt my attendance policy. Previously I had been quite rigid about class attendance. However, I have revised my policy to allow for two missed in-class exercises out of the fourteen that are conducted. The students have some flexibility in attendance with no penalty and may choose not to attend a class for very personal reasons.

Advance preparation for special events in class is also productive. I invite several resource visitors to class, such as a sexual abuse survivor, a person who has AIDS, a medical doctor, a sexual harassment counselor, and a panel of students from the Lesbian/Gay/Bisexual/Transgendered Alliance. If I prepare the students well ahead of time, they ask more in-depth questions and engage in thoughtful discussions. The visitors often comment on the respectful and courteous response of the students. Student course evaluations often reflect the positive impact these visitors had on their own perceptions.

Identifying Student Needs

Several recent initiatives in higher education emphasize reinforcing commitment to undergraduate instruction by becoming more student centered and focused on student learning. As professionals we are challenged to "address the academic and personal development of students in a holistic way" (Kellogg Commission, 1997, p. vi), to create student-centered learning environments (Palmer, 1998), to engage in active learning strategies that connect learning to real life (Donald, 1997), and to build communication skills through course work (Boyer Commission, 1998). Designing and implementing these initiatives is a continual challenge, especially to those of us who teach sensitive topics.

When teaching a very large class, many teachers find it difficult to assess individual student needs as they try to create a more student-centered learning environment. In order to assess the needs of students in my class better, I have developed an eighty-five-item personal sexuality profile. The questions are all multiple choice and cover the content that will be presented in class from a personal viewpoint. The topics range from frequency of sexual behaviors to types of sexual expression, to sexual orientation, to expressed values and attitudes, to contraceptive choices, to sexually transmitted diseases, to alcohol and drug use, to harassment, rape, and abuse issues—for example:

How important is love to you in a sexual relationship?
Very important   Important   Not important
Somewhat important   Unsure

Have you ever requested that a partner use sexually transmitted disease protection before engaging in sexual activity?
Yes   No   Does not apply

Have you ever consented to having sexual relations when you really didn't want to?
Many times   Often   Once or twice   Unsure
A few times   Never   Does not apply

The profile is administered to the students during the second week of class. The responses are anonymous and voluntary: however, I rarely have a student object to completing the survey. The answers are computer tabulated, and I report the relevant results to the students at the beginning of each new section of the course. I report the frequency of the total class responses to each item and the frequencies by male and female subgroups of the class. I find that the students show high interest in these results and are particularly interested in gender differences. The profile clearly demonstrates the diversity and pluralism represented in the class and clarifies misperceptions about many sexuality issues. It also helps class members to realize the range of experiences their classmates have had, which personalizes the course content. For example, 11 percent report having been raped, 13 percent report having had a sexually transmitted disease, 7 percent report being deeply religious, 25 percent report not having been sexually active in the past six months, 88 percent report that they want to have children, 6 percent believe abortion should not be legal under any circumstances, and 11 percent report that their parents were their main source of sexuality information.

Most important, the personal profile assists me in understanding the background experiences of the students and therefore informs my choice of course content and design. It helps me to approach topics with sensitivity and makes the issues vital and truly connected to the particular group of students I am teaching. Depending on the results of the profile, I may emphasize one area of content over another, or I may invite a resource visitor who can more appropriately address a particularly relevant issue. I work with the profile results throughout the semester and strongly believe it personalizes the large class.

Facilitating Open Conversation Within Boundaries

Because I value open communication, I strive to provide varied opportunities for the students to communicate with me or with the graduate assistants. Carbone (Chapter Four, this volume) suggests several techniques that have worked for her and other teachers of large classes. When sensitive issues are at center stage, I have found two techniques that work particularly well.

The Question/Comment Box. One of the most successful tools has been the use of the Question/Comment box. I place two open file boxes strategically in the classroom and encourage students to ask anonymous questions or make written comments about course content or procedures. I make a concerted effort to address these questions or comments at the beginning of the next lecture. Their offerings provide me with insight into what is important to them and also provides feedback on the success or failure of my methodologies. The questions range from specific medical concerns to sexual pleasuring techniques, to relationship issues, and to anecdotes that are relevant to their lives. Because so many of them are accustomed to an abusive, ill-informed talk show mentality related to personal issues, I feel it is important to respond with factual and accurate information. I also strive to model how to find reliable information or appropriate referrals if I do not know the answers. Initially, due to my students' personalized forthrightness and their expressed honest desire for basic sexual knowledge, many questions were difficult for me to answer. I shared that with the students. As I have gained confidence, I have found that researching the answers has taught me a great deal. I am also amazed at the wide range of issues that are of primary importance to the students. Among the hundreds of questions I have received, students have asked these:

- Can you get pregnant if you have sex in a hot tub?
- Is it rape if you ask the perpetrator to wear a condom?
- Where can I get an anonymous HIV test?

- I have genital herpes. Will I have to live with it forever?
- What are the dangers of anal sex?
- What effects does child sexual abuse have on sexual response later in life?
- I have a lump on my testicle. What could it be?
- How do you explain to a two year old that a penis is only for males? She thought hers was cut off.
- How can you tell if you really love someone or if it's just physical attraction?
- Does orange juice increase sperm count?
- Is homosexuality a learned behavior?
- Why do nice guys finish last?

Some students submit anecdotal references to situations they are facing. If they are appropriate, I may use them as a catalyst for class discussion or to introduce a new topic. I used the following anonymous anecdote to begin a discussion about setting sexual boundaries.

> When I am with a guy and we are both attracted to each other and he wants to have sex with me, but I don't want to, yet he continues to ask and is taking off his clothes and mine and he still wants to have sex, but I don't . . . he makes me feel guilty and so finally I give in and say yes. Is that OK? What could I have done or said besides "NO!"? He made me feel guilty. What can I do or say now?

This anecdote provided such good class discussion that I have incorporated it into an expanded, written in-class exercise so each student has the opportunity to respond individually before group discussion.

On rare occasion, a student has misused the Question/Comment box to submit a disrespectful or off-color comment. Although I may choose to ignore it, I usually address this issue directly with the class and again discuss scholarly integrity and respect. I feel strongly that the reason this technique has improved communication is because I devote time to it daily and the students frequently take advantage of the opportunity. Sometimes I receive far too many questions to cover. Then I explain that I will respond to only those questions that are not covered in the course content.

Some students are more comfortable communicating with me by e-mail. Although they lose their anonymity, e-mail offers them the opportunity for a personal response. I maintain strict adherence to confidentiality in order to protect the student and myself (Svinicki, 1994). Because of the large numbers of students and my time commitments, I do not encourage questions through e-mail, although I find it has been appropriate in most instances thus far. However, I felt that a professional boundary was crossed when one student chose repeatedly to share detailed accounts of how a priest had sexually abused her as a child and how she was now engaging in self-destructive behaviors. I felt that the student needed more than I was prepared to offer. Whether we are communicating by e-mail or in person, it is important for me to distinguish clearly between my role as an educator and the very different role of a counselor.

Because of the personalized nature of the course content, I am frequently the first person to whom the student has chosen to reveal his or her story. If I judge that the student is sharing confidential information that is beyond my comfort level, I quickly share my compassion but clearly set a boundary. I explain that it would be best if the student pursued this matter with a professional counselor, and I keep my office well supplied with brochures and telephone numbers. Once when I felt a student was dangerous to herself, I accompanied her directly to the counselor's office after making telephone arrangements. For obvious reasons, it is imperative that teachers who address sensitive academic content that can become highly personalized also set clear personal and professional boundaries.

Student Representative Group. Because it is often difficult to get direct feedback from students in a large class, I have periodically formed a volunteer student representative group. I ask for student volunteers who will meet with me and the graduate teaching assistants every two weeks for one hour after class. I usually get a group of twelve to fifteen students to volunteer after I promise a reward of a pizza supper at the end of the semester. The purpose of the group is to facilitate class management, help make decisions regarding class content, provide student input into class procedures to offer direct feedback, and solve problems. These informal meetings offer an excellent opportunity for me to have small group interaction and open discussion about the class. At every other meeting, the graduate teaching assistants meet alone with the group in order to get honest yet somewhat anonymous feedback about my teaching methodology. The graduate assistants have also conducted in-depth case studies of a selection of students to ascertain the impact of the course. This is an effective way to increase the responsibilities of the graduate teaching assistants while engaging them in direct interactions with the students.

This group has been a valuable resource to inform my teaching style. I ask for their advice about the pacing of the class and the order of the topics addressed. I receive helpful feedback. For example, they like it when I walk around the room and have direct eye contact with them. They tell me it is fine to share my values but not to preach them. In a course that has much value-laden content, it is important that I model the best scholarly and ethical standards and not promote my own personal philosophy (Svinicki, 1994). It is important to them that I set classroom limits the first day and enforce them. I have asked the student volunteers how to handle disciplinary issues in the classroom, such as people talking in the back row or someone who dominates the discussions. They are usually candid in their suggestions, and invariably they prefer that I deal directly with disruptive students by confronting them. In fact, I have had members of the student representative group volunteer to talk individually with students who may be causing a problem in the class.

I ask the student group to offer feedback on the use of materials in the class, such as the relevance of the textbook and the clarity of the overheads. I have asked them to preview and critique new videos that I felt could be potentially offensive. They have also recommended resource visitors to address specific issues for the course. I often rehearse a new interactive activity I am planning with this group and benefit from their suggestions. Sometimes the group proposes an idea for an in-class activity to address an issue of concern.

The most important outcome for me is that this group of students has helped me immensely with sensitive issues. The group offers the student perspective and often suggests alternatives that would never occur to me. The students are a rich source of ideas for how to prepare the class for a sensitive topic. They also provide a sounding board for me when I am processing an occurrence in the classroom. Their perspective has often enlightened and humbled me. Because I introduce these students to the total class and identify them as volunteer student representatives, I find that other students bring concerns to them that they might have been reluctant to bring directly to me. This obviously improves the communication between students and the instructor in a large lecture class, especially when the class is highly charged with sensitive content.

Assignments That Help Students Process Sensitive Issues

Because the nature of the content of the human sexuality course is personal and intimate, I design a variety of assignments that will help students in integrating knowledge with their personal lives and applying knowledge to their decision making and problem solving.

Research and Writing Exercises. All of the students complete a study guide that corresponds to the textbook chapters. The personal study provides good review of content and incorporates personal responses to relevant issues. Due to the sensitive nature of many of the study guide items, I provide flexibility in assigning the work. I require the students to complete all of the activities that relate to learning content, but I ask them to choose only two personalized activities to complete from the remaining four or five chapter activities. This instruction allows the students options and latitude when they are processing personal and sensitive issues. The students are evaluated on the comprehensiveness and completeness of their answers but are not judged on their stated values and personal interpretations. We expect a variety of responses; however, we clearly ask that personal opinions be stated in a respectful manner.

I also implement fourteen interactive, written, cooperative-learning exercises that are completed during class time. These exercises are designed to integrate personal values and course content. I evaluate the amount of effort put into the exercise and the quality of the written response. Again, I encourage diverse, personal opinions and reactions as long as they are stated in a respectful manner. These activities, varied in nature, provide another option for students to express themselves in a personal yet safe manner. In-class activities are unannounced and are designed to provide students an opportunity to respond personally to sensitive issues ranging from sexuality education of children to

disabilities, to sexual arousal, to sexual orientation. Often I present an anecdote, and each student writes a personal response to the problem that it poses.
Then the students discuss their responses in small groups, followed by a large
class discussion. Here are two examples of these anecdotal problems:

> During Thanksgiving holiday while relatives are visiting, your sister is six
> months pregnant. You have a five year old who is quite interested in your sis-
> ter's "large 'tummy.'" You explain that your sister is going to have a baby. Later
> that week while you are putting your child to bed, your child asks you how the
> baby got inside Aunt Jeanne's tummy. How would you answer?

> Your college roommate seems to know it all. During a late-night discussion your
> roommate tells you: "If you're having trouble loosening up in a new relationship,
> just start drinking alcohol, and after a few drinks all your cares go away and
> you're just into the sex for you. I guess you don't care much about the person
> you're with except to get what it is you need to satisfy yourself. Besides, every-
> body is doing it." What are the facts of this situation? What are your feelings?
> What do you do and/or say to your roommate?

On the last day of class I ask the students to evaluate how the objectives
of the class were met and then ask each to write his or her own personal bill
of sexual rights. It is my goal that this activity will help them to synthesize what
they have learned and then apply it to their own lives.

Service-Learning. Service-learning provides another occasion for application of learning. As Kuh, Douglas, Lund, and Ramin-Gyurnek (1994) wrote,
"Colleges and universities can no longer afford to ignore the rich potential of
out-of-class experiences in fostering student learning" (p. 47). Although I have
not formalized the opportunity in the class, I believe that involvement in service-learning experiences in the community helps students integrate sensitive
course content with real-life issues.

In the course syllabus I encourage students to volunteer with the campus
peer health educators, the peer substance abuse prevention organization, and
the student health advisory committee. I also encourage involvement with the
local AIDS Coalition, the Youth and Shelter Services, and the Assault Care Center Extending Shelter and Support. I provide contact people, telephone numbers, and dates of training programs for volunteers. Many students from the
course become involved in efforts to advance sexuality education in the community by volunteering their time. I hope to formalize the students' involvement
in out-of-class activities in the near future. These real-life activities help the students to apply their knowledge and offer direct interaction with sensitive issues.

Conclusion

Teachers are explorers. As they explore the world and the lives of their students, they cast lines to different ways of thinking. Teaching is often bridge
building. Beginning on one shore with the knowledge, experience, know-how,

and interests of the student, the teacher moves toward broader horizons and deeper ways of knowing (Ayers, 1993, p. 66).

Teaching a class that is highly charged with sensitive issues has been a journey of exploration for me. I have learned deeper ways of knowing about establishing ground rules for respect, setting limits on behavior, implementing interactive learning techniques, designing curriculum based on students' needs and interests, and encouraging open communication in a large class. But as Parker Palmer states, "Good teaching cannot be reduced to technique: good teaching comes from the identity and integrity of the teacher" (1997, p. 16). By accepting the challenge to educate students about sensitive issues relevant to their personal choices, I have broadened my own horizons and become a partner in learning. If we are to create holistic, student-centered learning environments and take student learning seriously, scholarly attention must be given to the sensitive issues affecting our students' lives.

References

Ayers, W. *To Teach: The Journey of a Teacher*. New York: Teachers College Press, 1993.

Boyer Commission on Educating Undergraduates in the Research University. *Reinventing Undergraduate Education: A Blueprint for America's Research Universities*. Menlo Park, Calif.: Carnegie Foundation for the Advancement of Teaching, 1998.

Brookfield, S. D. *The Skillful Teacher*. San Francisco: Jossey-Bass, 1990.

Donald, J. *Improving the Environment for Learning: Academic Leaders Talk About What Works*. San Francisco: Jossey-Bass, 1997.

Kellogg Commission on the Future of State and Land-Grant Universities. *Returning to Our Roots: The Student Experience*. Washington, D.C.: National Association of State Universities and Land-Grant Colleges, 1997.

Keltner, J. W. "Views from Different Sides of the Desk: Conflict Between Faculty and Students." In S. A Holton (ed.), *Mending the Cracks in the Ivory Tower*. Bolton, Mass.: Anker, 1998.

Kuh, G. D., Douglas, K. B., Lund, J. P., and Ramin-Gyurnek, J. *Student Learning Outside the Classroom*. ASHE-ERIC Higher Education Report, no. 8. Washington, D.C.: School of Education and Human Development, George Washington University, 1994.

Levine, A., and Cureton, J. S. "Collegiate Life: An Obituary." *Change*, 1998, *30* (3), 12–17.

Maddock, J. W. (ed.). *Sexuality Education in Postsecondary and Professional Training Settings*. New York: Haworth Press, 1997.

Palmer P. J. "The Heart of a Teacher: Identity and Integrity in Teaching." *Change*, Nov.–Dec. 1997, pp. 15–21.

Palmer, P. J. *The Courage to Teach*. San Francisco: Jossey-Bass, 1998.

Schneider, A. "Insubordination and Intimidation Signal the End of Decorum in Many Classrooms." *Chronicle of Higher Education*, Mar. 27, 1998, pp. A12–A14.

Strong, B., and DeVault, C. *Human Sexuality: Diversity in Contemporary America*. Mountain View, Calif.: Mayfield, 1997.

Svinicki, M. "Ethics in College Teaching." In W. J. McKeachie (ed.), *Teaching Tips: Strategies, Research and Theory for College and University Teachers*. (9th ed.) Lexington, Mass.: Heath, 1994.

Tierney, W. G. *Building Communities of Difference: Higher Education in the Twenty-First Century*. New York: Bergin & Garvey, 1993.

CORLY PETERSEN BROOKE *is director for the Center for Teaching Excellence and professor of human development and family studies at Iowa State University.*

Experienced faculty have come up with excellent ideas for solving the
discipline problems that plague large classes.

Students Behaving Badly in
Large Classes

Elisa Carbone

A few months ago I received an e-mail from a faculty member: "Could we meet to discuss some problems I'm having in my large class?" She went on to list some of her areas of concern: how to set up group work, how to deal with exam logistics, and so on. She came to the Center for Teaching Excellence to meet with director Jim Greenberg and me, and after we had brainstormed some ideas about group work and exams, the real problem surfaced: the students in her large class were behaving abominably. They wandered in late, left early, read the newspaper, chatted with friends during the lecture, and napped; not surprisingly, a large number of them were failing the course. It was her first semester teaching a large class. She never wanted to do it again.

In addition to these problems, faculty generally have found that large classes have poorer attendance, louder packing up of books a few minutes before the end of class, more cheating on exams, and more off-task behavior during discussions and group activities. They also report a startling array of innovative disruptive behaviors during class, including talking on cell phones, watching portable televisions, sitting through the lecture with headphones on, having pizza delivered during the middle of class, fraternity pledges' pretending to have a nervous breakdown during an exam, and passionate making out in the back of the classroom.

This incivility seems to be caused by the same mind-set that allows otherwise polite individuals to gesture rudely at other motorists in a traffic jam or shout obscenities at a referee at a crowded sporting event. The anonymity and impersonal nature of a large class can inspire students to behavior they would never dream of exhibiting in their small classes.

NEW DIRECTIONS FOR TEACHING AND LEARNING, no. 77, Spring 1999 © Jossey-Bass Publishers

Concern over student behavior is often at the top of the list among teachers of large classes. It is demeaning and disheartening to have a lecture ignored in favor of chitchat or to have students milling into and out of the lecture hall as if it were a hotel lobby. How can we encourage civility in the large classroom? How can we as faculty stay in control of large numbers of students so that the class time is respected?

Setting Clear Expectations Up Front

There is no one right answer to the question of how much control to exert over the students in a large class. Each faculty member must decide what kinds of behaviors are acceptable in his or her classroom and what kinds of behaviors are intolerable. Do you not mind a few latecomers as long as they take their seats quietly? Or would you rather students not come at all if they cannot get there on time? Control styles range from authoritarian to laissez-faire. An authoritarian lecturer is likely to march up the aisle toward a student who is about to leave early and ask him, in front of five hundred of his peers, where he is going. The laissez-faire lecturer often does not mind side talking, newspaper reading, or other errant behavior as long as it takes place in the upper tiers of the lecture hall and is not a distraction to the students who have chosen to sit up front (Carbone, 1998). And many faculty fall somewhere in between these two ends of the spectrum.

It is important to determine what you expect of your students before the first day of class, so that on that first day you communicate these expectations firmly and clearly. Robin Sawyer (Department of Health Education, University of Maryland) spent many years teaching middle school and high school before joining the faculty at the University of Maryland. He says that in many ways, college students are just big high school students. The twenty minutes he spends going over class rules on the first day of class remind him of his days in public school, but, he says, "It saves me incredible grief down the road." He has found an exponential decrease in behavior problems that stems from expressing his expectations on the first day of class. "You wouldn't think you'd have to talk about these things to twenty-one-year-old college students," he says, "but you do."

I spoke with Rachel, a freshman at a large university where every one of her classes has over two hundred students. She says she and her fellow students are happy to live up to teachers' expectations for conduct, but want to know about these expectations at the outset. In one of Rachel's classes the teacher has just started, in midsemester, to berate students for being late. "She never said anything about how she wanted people to come in on time, and now she's telling us she had this expectation and we're getting yelled at for it," said Rachel. She has noticed that the teacher's anger, along with the students' feeling that they were not forewarned, has damaged the rapport in the class. If you are reading this and thinking, "But students should know that coming in late is rude!" think again. Some teachers do not mind lateness and never show annoyance over it. They feel as though students are paying for the class, they may have to travel a long way across campus from a previous class or come to class straight from a job, and their lateness is their own business. Many students agree with this sentiment. The only way for students to know if they have landed in a class where lateness (or any other behavior) will not be tolerated is for this expectation to be laid out clearly.

It does not hurt to repeat the rules of conduct on the second day of class (since some of the students who most need to hear them may not have shown up on the first day) and periodically throughout the semester, especially if students seem to be forgetting them. It is also helpful to include your expectations in the syllabus, so students will come across them when double-checking the due date for a paper. Jack Osman (Department of Health Science, Towson University) hands out with the syllabus a separate sheet of behavioral expectations, which include his rules about tardiness, attendance, classroom conduct, and cheating. Each student is required to sign a statement at the bottom of this sheet that he or she has read the list and agrees to abide by the rules. It is not a contract, since Osman does not countersign, and he does not collect them but requires students to keep them in their notebooks. If a problem arises, Osman calls students' attention to the list and their signature and reminds an offending student that he or she has made a commitment to behave otherwise.

Tara Torchia (Department of Health Education, University of Maryland) notes that when laying down the law on that first day of class, it is important not only to tell students how you expect them to act but also to explain why. "It's not just, 'Because I told you so and I'm the teacher,'" says Torchia. She lets them know that she wants no side conversations, no one coming in late or leaving early, and no one reading the newspaper "because it's distracting to me and to other students." Giving them an explanation is part of setting a tone of respect, says Torchia. She also gets students to agree to codes of conduct. On the first day of class she asks them if they think one minute is enough time for them to pack up their notebooks and backpacks before leaving for their next class. "Does anyone think that's not enough time?" she asks. Once students have agreed that they can complete this noisy task in one minute, she promises to let them out one minute early each class, so that the commotion of packing up will not interfere with her lecture. If she then notices the beginnings of noise before this one-minute cutoff, she looks at her watch and says, "It doesn't look like time to pack up to me." Students quiet down and wait for her signal. Torchia says that giving students explanations and asking them for their agreement with behavior codes lets them know that they too must take responsibility for creating a positive learning environment in the classroom.

Student Opinions on Classroom Discipline

One faculty member shared this story with me: She was teaching a large class in which two male students consistently engaged in side talking. After several class periods, she finally asked one of the students to move to the other side of the room. He did so, walking on the tops of the desks as he went. The professor was so stunned that she did not know what to do. As a result, she did nothing. The boys shaped up a bit but continued to be somewhat of a disruption problem for the rest of the semester. In her end-of-semester evaluations, this faculty member received numerous comments about the incident, such as, "We were all embarrassed by how those students behaved. You should have kicked them out," and "You shouldn't have let those students be that disruptive." It became quite clear that the class felt she should have been more forceful in controlling disruptive student behavior.

Although some forms of misbehavior, such as working crossword puzzles or napping, are more distracting to the professor than to other students, there seems to be a general feeling among students that they appreciate it when instructors control noisy behavior. In a questionnaire administered at the University of Washington, students were asked what hindered their learning in large classes. One of the most often cited problems was the behavior of their fellow students—specifically side conversations, arriving late, and leaving early (Wulff, Nyquist, and Abbott, 1987). In a study of large classes conducted by Amy Allen (Department of Nutrition and Food Science, University of Maryland) students wrote the following comments in their end-of-semester evaluations: "Freshmen behave like they're on a chicken farm. It takes them ten minutes to settle down and they become restless ten minutes before the class ends," and "These students are awful. They're loud, disrespectful and totally uninterested. I want to line them all up and beat them with a fire hose" (Allen, 1998). Allen found that in classes where faculty did not regularly address side talking, there was a strong response from students indicating that they felt the noise level was unacceptable.

When you take steps to control student behavior in your large classroom, you are not doing it only for yourself. There is a large silent majority of students who want to spend their time listening rather than being distracted by a handful of rowdy classmates.

Teachers Taking Responsibility

Torchia takes a proactive approach to student incivility in her large classes. She takes on the responsibility of making her classes so interesting and challenging that students want to be there and pay attention. To do this, she uses a number of devices to spice up her lectures: visuals, stories, personal references, props, guest speakers, active learning, and even music that relates to her lecture material. "I take the approach that you have to look at it as theater," says Torchia. "You wouldn't put on a play by standing next to an overhead with the lights turned down."

Torchia finds that moving around the room helps to keep students in every part of the lecture hall tuned in to her. She places visuals all around the room and moves to them as she lectures. "Students do have to turn around in order to see," she says, "but if you're turning around to look, you're going to be paying attention."

It is also important for faculty to teach by example. If you want to encourage students not to be late, arrive a few minutes early and start class exactly on time. And, most important, if you want students to demonstrate respect for you and for the class time, show respect to them. I recently came across a syllabus that, in an ill-guided attempt to stop students from side talking, stated, essentially, "The people sitting near you are not interested in your personal life. . . . Idle chitchat is immature behavior." It went on for several more sentences about how annoying and uninteresting side conversations are. It is not surprising that the strongly worded syllabus did not achieve its goal of curtailing side conversations. The syllabus is asking for civility in a manner that is demeaning and uncivil. Students read this syllabus at the start of the semester, before any of them had engaged in side conversations, and they were already being insulted. If we want students to act like adults, or at least more like adults, we need to treat them with the kind of respect we offer adults.

Personalizing the Large Class

Students behave in large classes in ways they never would in small classes. Many students find from the start that the impersonal nature of large classes is alienating, and their uncivil behavior is often an offshoot of this alienation. Making a large class more personal can ameliorate this situation. Maryellen Gleason (1986) suggests treating the large class as if it were a small class. In other words, behave as you would in your classes of twenty-five or thirty: come in early and chat with a few students, when a student asks a question move closer as you answer it, stay after class to talk with interested students, make an effort to learn as many names as possible, and choose twenty or so exams or papers from each batch graded by your teaching assistants and write personal comments on them.

Denny Gulick (Department of Mathematics, University of Maryland) holds a weekly workshop session for his students. This session is not required, but it offers students a chance for more personal interaction with him. About twenty to thirty students attend each week, and the response has been very positive. Students appreciate both the chance to review the material and the more personal tone these meetings bring to Gulick's large lecture class. "This is my way of walking halfway to them," says Gulick.

It is not possible to meet with each student in a large class individually, but there are ways to hear from individuals in the class and respond to them. The one-minute paper is an excellent way to find out how students are handling the material, hear what questions they have, and be able to give personal feedback to several students each time the papers are collected (Angelo and Cross, 1993).

William Harwood (Department of Chemistry and Biochemistry, University of Maryland) uses the one-minute paper in his Introductory Chemistry and General Chemistry courses early in the semester and then periodically throughout the semester. He stops class a few minutes early and asks students to write down any questions they still have concerning the material covered in class. Participation is voluntary, and there are drop boxes stationed around the room. At the beginning of the following class session, Harwood chooses several of the questions to answer for the whole class. He finds that his responsiveness to their questions, and the chance for students to have their own questions answered, helps to establish a positive and personal classroom rapport. "One of the things that is difficult for students in a large class is to ask questions," says Harwood. "They are afraid of how they will appear to their peers." He says that the one-minute paper gives students a chance to ask their questions anonymously. And when a question is answered in front of the whole class, it gives validation to anyone who asked that question or a similar one. "When they see my respectful response to their questions, this sends a powerful message that I listen to their voices," says Harwood. He also finds that after a few weeks of using the one-minute paper, students are much more willing to raise their hands and ask their questions during class. Consequently the number of questions in the drop boxes goes down, and there is more oral class participation.

These suggestions are not particularly time-consuming, and they can make a big difference in how alienating or welcoming a large class feels to students. These types of personalizing behaviors on the part of faculty can help create an atmosphere that is more conducive to civility overall.

Some Questionable Practices

There are some other ways to control student behavior, and each faculty member must weigh the pros and cons of using them. For example, one way to encourage students to attend class, get there on time, and stay until the end of the class period is to give a pop quiz or other surprise in-class written assignment each week, sometimes at the beginning of class and sometimes at the end. This offers a form of extra credit to students who are present because students who are not there get a zero. Unfortunately, this strategy will cause more uninterested students to attend class simply so that they will be there when the pop quiz appears. You may therefore end up with a louder, more disruptive class and with more students working crossword puzzles during your lecture because the only reason they are there is to get the extra points.

Another example is the use of assigned seats, usually with students sitting in their discussion sections. This allows teaching assistants to take attendance and can make it easy to deduct points for poor attendance, thus encouraging good attendance. It also cuts down on side talking because students are separated from their friends. But, notes Amy Allen, assigned seating is unfair to those dedicated students who would normally come twenty minutes early to class to get a front-row seat. About these strategies designed to control the behavior of less motivated students, Allen says, "I wouldn't sacrifice my A students to get through to my D students."

To Embarrass or Not to Embarrass?

Yank the student newspaper out of his hands or speak to him about his rude behavior after class? Tell the three girls chatting in the fifth row that everyone around them is giving them dirty looks, so hush up, or simply move into their personal space as a hint to stop chatting? Some faculty use public embarrassment as a deterrent to uncivil behavior, and say that once one student has been embarrassed, it is very unlikely that another student will commit the same offense. Other faculty find public embarrassment distasteful and would rather speak to an errant student in private.

Tara Torchia does not believe in public embarrassment and uses alternative methods for controlling student behavior. For example, if a student has been late several times, she will ask the student to see her after class. She asks him or her, "What is making you arrive late? Do you have another class? Are you having trouble getting up in the morning?" She then goes on to stress that walking in late is distracting to her and the other students, and she has gone as far as suggesting that if waking up on time is the problem, the student switch to an afternoon section of the class. For side talkers, she addresses them pleasantly, saying, "You're probably talking about something really interesting related to the lecture, and maybe we can talk more about it after class, but for right now let's focus on what we're doing here." These gentle nudges create order in her classroom in a way she is comfortable with.

Jack Osman uses what he calls "gracious public embarrassment" and finds it very effective: late students are regularly required to become part of the lecture before they take their seats. As a consequence very few students walk in late. "It is done with humor, and with love," says Osman, "but they know it means something. Here is an example: It is ten after two in the afternoon, and Osman's class began at two o'clock. He is lecturing on the effects of drunk driving and the penalties for drunk driving in a number of different countries. A student, a girl with blonde hair pulled back in a short ponytail, walks into the lecture hall. Osman stops her and asks her name. It is Christina. She is now standing at the front of the lecture hall with Osman, facing the tiers filled with students. "Christina," Osman addresses her in his lecture voice, "if you were out partying and were the one driving, and you had a couple of extra drinks, what would you do?" Christina gives the correct answer: call a cab or give her keys to a friend who has not been drinking. But it is not time for her to sit down yet. "Christina, have you traveled outside of the United States?" Osman asks. She has. "Where?" he wants to know. We hear briefly about Christina's travel history and learn what the penalties are for drunk drivers in San Salvador, Turkey, and Saudi Arabia before Christina, smiling sheepishly with her shoulders hunched over her books, is allowed to sit down.

Rick, a senior, says he appreciates Osman's good-humored methods. "He makes you laugh," says Rick, "and it's better than the way a lot of professors deal with it." Rick described an incident that had happened the previous week in another class. He walked into a class four minutes late, and the professor screamed at him and told him to get out. "The unprofessionalism was terrible," said Rick. "It was disgusting." Not only had the professor reduced his rapport with his students, but he had damaged his own credibility in their eyes.

Denny Gulick also uses gentle public embarrassment, "politely, with levity and with a smile." A student fell asleep in one of his classes recently. Gulick addressed the class, saying, "Oh my gosh, that person fell asleep! What should we do?" Everyone looked around, the commotion woke the person up, and Gulick went on with his lecture. When students are side talking, Gulick addresses them and asks if they have a question about the material. "I call attention to their behavior in a way that makes it clear I'm not dumping on them as people, but I'm dumping on the fact that they haven't been conscientious," says Gulick. "We need to make the environment the best we can for those who want to learn. So controlling student behavior isn't a negative, it becomes a positive."

Cheating

Cheating is a concern in any classroom, and for large classes the problem seems to be multiplied. Teachers rely more on multiple-choice tests, and it is difficult to watch the eyes of five hundred students. In addition the sheer number of papers combined with the fact that papers are often graded by several different teaching assistants makes it almost impossible to detect when a paper has been lifted from a past class. There are the classic rules that faculty use to deter cheating during exams: separate students as much as possible, every-other-row seating with different forms of the test, baseball caps must be turned backward (those brims can hide wandering eyes), and no sunglasses. I also came across several ingenious methods faculty are using to deter cheating on both exams and on papers.

Jack Osman has come up with a variation on the idea of different forms of a multiple-choice exam that is much easier and every bit as effective. He uses the same exam for all students but creates two answer keys. On one answer key the question numbers are listed vertically, and on the other they are listed horizontally. It is simple, saves paperwork, and makes it virtually impossible for students to cheat because the answer key next to them is too visually confusing and different from their own.

With fraternities and sororities keeping files of papers for their members to use and now with the Internet offering an extensive array of writing from various classes for students to lift and put their name on, papers are not at all cheatproof. To counteract this, Sharon Hollander (Department of Education, College of Staten Island) uses memoirs—different ones each semester—to inspire original student papers. Students pick one of the two memoirs to read and write about. This semester they had the choice of *Let Me Hear Your Voice* by Catherine Maurice or *The Broken Cord* by Michael Dorris, both about the family lives of disabled children. Next semester there will be two different books to pick from, probably about a slightly different topic in the field of psychology. "I have a myriad of memoirs to choose from," says Hollander. She says that when students write their papers, "they can't copy from another [past] student, they can't recycle from another class, and they can't lift it off the Internet or out of some other source." In addition, Hollander finds that the personal nature of the memoirs themselves inspires students to read them, connect them to their own lives, and write reflective, original papers.

Conclusion: Moral Development

John Zacker (associate director of judicial programs, University of Maryland) sees the students who have taken a giant step across the line of misbehavior. He gets to know the students who, for example, have tried to steal books from the library or have forged a doctor's note for missed exams. He considers the mission of his office not just that of punishing and sanctioning errant students but of helping these students develop a stronger moral sense. And he invites all faculty to join in this mission. "I think that this discussion of student moral and civil behavior is terribly important for all of us. We all have a great deal of contact with our students, and to be able to understand not only their intellectual development but also understand their human and moral development will only help us to educate our students to be better citizens."

Think of the time and attention you dedicate to promoting civility in your large classroom as more than housekeeping. Think of it as part of what you are teaching.

References

Allen, A. "Lecture Size and Its Relationship to Student Performance, Attitudes and Behavior and Faculty Attitudes and Behavior in a College-Level Introductory Nutrition Course." Unpublished doctoral dissertation, Department of Nutrition, University of Maryland, 1998.

Angelo, T. A., and Cross, K. P. *Classroom Assessment Techniques.* (2nd ed.) San Francisco: Jossey-Bass, 1993.

Carbone, E. *Teaching Large Classes: Tools and Strategies.* Thousand Oaks, Calif.: Sage, 1998.

Gleason, M. "Better Communication in Large Courses." *College Teaching,* 1986, 34 (1), 20–24.

Wulff, D. H., Nyquist, J. D., and Abbott, R. D. "Students' Perceptions of Large Classes." In M. G. Weimer (ed.), *Teaching Large Classes Well.* New Directions for Teaching and Learning, no. 32. San Francisco: Jossey-Bass, 1987.

ELISA CARBONE is a lecturer in speech communication at the University of Maryland University College. From 1995 to 1998 she was coordinator of the Large Classes Project for the Center for Teaching Excellence at the University of Maryland.

Teachers may use a variety of strategies for understanding and dealing with difficult behavior.

Strategies for Dealing with Difficult Behavior

Sally L. Kuhlenschmidt, Lois E. Layne

We may imagine ourselves to be sage professors with rapt students hanging on our every word; however, the reality of classroom life may be very different. All faculty are confronted with students who engage in behaviors that are disruptive to the educational process. Students may be late for class, leave early, talk inappropriately, or sleep during class. Recently faculty have reported more threatening behaviors, including stalking, intimidation, physical or verbal attacks, and "hijacking" classrooms (Schneider, 1998). If ignored or handled poorly, even a single act of incivility can have a long-term impact on classroom atmosphere. Misbehavior may escalate to intolerable or dangerous levels. Following is a problem-solving strategy for dealing with disruptive student behavior, based on clinical and classroom experience.

The approach uses a series of steps or questions designed to provide perspective on the problem behavior and aid in generating responses. The first questions are concerned with clarifying the problem, identifying critical elements, describing the context in which the behavior occurs, and analyzing your emotional and behavioral responses to the behavior. Next, we review factors that might contribute to disruptive classroom behavior. Once the situation is fully understood, the final steps are to select a response and evaluate the effectiveness of the strategy. The steps can be followed like a checklist. The process of checking off the steps or questions can be repeated with new problem situations until the process is second nature.

Describing the Problem Clearly

Jumping to conclusions about the source and nature of a problem is a recipe for failure. Becoming irritated or highly emotional may lead you to react without understanding the situation. Disruptive student behavior may have nothing to do with the instructor or the class. Instructors tend to personalize the behavior, however, feeling that they did something to cause a student to react. Evaluating behavior before taking action is a skill that takes practice and reflection. You may feel pressure to handle the problem behavior immediately. Taking the time to understand the behavior and to consider various options often results in a more constructive resolution. After an event is past, taking time to evaluate the effectiveness of your response can help to improve your reaction in the next situation.

Ideally you would answer the following questions about a situation before taking action. There will be times, however, when delay is not desirable. For example, if emotional agitation escalates rather than reduces with time and discussion, then your immediate professional intervention may be best.

What Is the Behavior? What Is the Situation? Behavior is that which can be directly sensed, such as seen or heard. Often people's "descriptions" of behavior include inferences ("He was aggressive," "She is lazy"). Instead, describe the behavior itself. Say, "He kicked the chair" rather than "He was aggressive" or "She turned in only one of five assignments" rather than "She was lazy." The problem with inference is that it includes the prescription before the facts are known and allows for misinterpretation. In one case we know of, instructors regarded a grossly overweight student as behaviorally disruptive in class. His actual in-class behavior was within normal ranges, but the instructors made false generalizations from his physical appearance. The inverse problem is also common. A very attractive student may be given more leeway than is appropriate, encouraging misbehavior in other students. Examine the labels you give to students, and rephrase them as objective behaviors rather than categories. Objective behaviors can be recorded by an inanimate recording device, such as a video camera. If you have trouble with rephrasing, you might be making an inference.

When Does It Happen? Behavior is often time dependent. Time patterns may suggest possible solutions or clues for why the behavior is occurring. For example, lateness, by definition, occurs near the beginning of class and may be due to another instructor's dismissing class late. Disruptive talking may be more common near the end of class. Planning a small group activity in the latter half of class may reduce restlessness. Students who are sitting next to friends are more likely to chat. Using a seating chart may reduce extraneous chatting and help you to know your students by name, further reducing disruption.

What Is Going on Before, During, and After the Behavior? Behavior typically occurs because of some environmental signal or because the behavior has been rewarded in the past. When exams or assignments are returned, students are more likely to speak out, for example. If grading criteria or remarks are vague, there is more room for disaffection. If the instructor bends the rules for one student and others see, then they may demand similar treatment. Is the problem behavior the result of unclear or inappropriate signals?

The consequences that a student experiences during and following a behavior influence her future ways of responding. A student may have received teacher attention in high school for making remarks regardless of their relevance. Now the student frequently mentions irrelevant material. Is the college instructor encouraging this problem behavior to continue with smiles or nods or further questions?

Consequences can also work to eliminate desirable behavior. If students are silent but you want discussion, what is discouraging that behavior? Are you making remarks that could be interpreted as critical of those who speak?

Who Is Involved or Affected? A behavior may be annoying to you, but other students may not notice it. Or students may be bothered by something you have not seen. If you are the only one annoyed, reexamine your assumptions about what must and must not happen in a classroom. Perhaps the behavior is not as serious as you believe. Conversely if a considerable portion of the class is bothered and you do not address the need, then you lose some ability to manage the classroom.

Although only the students and instructors are present, relationships and events outside the classroom (for example, the death of a family member, being stalked by an ex-boyfriend, or falling in love) may have an impact on a student's classroom behavior. Be alert to cultural differences in what constitutes a significant relationship. For example, relationships with siblings and roommates can be very important to students. The classroom instructor is not and should not act as a therapist. Delicate questioning may be sufficient to reveal that the source of the problem lies outside your purview (try saying, for example, "I noticed you seem distracted in class. Is everything okay?"). You and the student can then move on to determining how to avoid having the outside issue affect classroom behavior. Often nonjudgmental listening is enough, with a referral to local campus and community resources for counseling if it seems warranted. Ask your local counseling center if it will share its list of referral sources.

Is the Behavior Harmful to the Student, to You, or to Others? The ideal is to prevent threatening behavior from ever occurring. It is important to notice the early signs and redirect the energy or address the problem as soon as possible. Such things as clear instructions and appropriate instructor behavior can help avoid many unpleasant situations.

Sometimes a potentially harmful situation develops despite your efforts. If you detect high-risk behaviors such as drinking and driving, promiscuity, or eating disorders, you should be concerned and consider referral. How do you determine danger? No one is very good at it. In general, a history of harmful behavior is the best predictor, coupled with a clear plan to commit harm. There is a range of potentially harmful situations, from a vague threat of suicide to a student walking into class with a gun. The more concrete and immediate the threat is, the more urgently that expert intervention is needed.

Delaying action is not appropriate when harm is imminent. If a student shares her concern with you, it is typically a sign she wants help. There is a limit, however, to the help you can and should provide. Seek professional advice on how to obtain professional intervention for the student. Ideally the dean of students, mental health counseling personnel, and the campus police work together and have a response for potentially harmful situations. The time to learn if such a plan exists is now, not when you have a student in danger. Take the time to learn whether your institution has a policy for evicting students who are threatening. Record the telephone numbers of appropriate services in an easily accessible location (the bottom of the telephone perhaps). Our university's faculty development center provides a door hanger to new faculty with basic referral sources and telephone numbers. Finally, if a dangerous situation does arise, document your interactions in case there is a need for a record of your involvement. Avoid making inferential statements in the document.

How Do You Feel About the Behavior? If you are upset about an incident and fail to acknowledge your emotional reaction, you will be a poor problem solver (see Chapter Two, this volume). Heightened emotion interferes with problem solving and the capacity to generate multiple effective solutions. A teacher who is upset is likely to say or do things that escalate the problem and alienate students and administrators. For example, if you feel that a student's behavior is a personal attack on you (and even if it is), you may be tempted to regain control by getting tough or intimidating the student. Counteraggression will not usually solve a problem, and it often buys into the conscious or subconscious desires of the student. You will end up reacting to the student rather than making a proactive decision. A strong personal reaction calls for a cooling-off period before taking action. If you are tired or burned out, do not deal with the problem until you are emotionally able. It is better to acknowledge the student's anger and suggest that the two of you approach the problem at a specific later time. To avoid the student's suspicion that you are merely putting him off, demonstrate your commitment to that appointment by writing it in your schedule.

Another question you should ask at this point is, "What have I contributed to the disruptive incident?" Instructors typically perceive their behavior to be reasonable and appropriate. The power differential existing between instructors and students, however, suggests that what may appear unimportant to you could be very painful to the student. You will be a better mediator if you examine your behavior from the perspective of the student (see Chapter Eight, this volume). Examining your behavior includes knowing that you cannot always be objective and may need to seek an honest outside opinion, not merely a supporting opinion. Instructors who can recognize a true error and correct it will likely have better student relations.

What Changes Would Make the Behavior or Situation Acceptable? Often people try to change a situation without knowing their objectives. They simply want something different. The consequence may be directions to students that are vague, confusing, and contradictory, resulting in further unsatisfactory behavior. If you are clear about desired behavior, then students can comply more readily. Balance clarity with giving students choices. Students also like to feel in control and tend to take more responsibility when they make the initial choice.

Giving effective directions is difficult to do well. Examples of common but vague instructions include these: "Contribute to class interaction" or "Good." Effective directions are specific in terms of the target behaviors (for example, try saying, "Offer a question, an opinion with an example, or a response to another student's statement"). Effective directions are also specific about the amount of behavior (for example, "On discussion days offer at least one comment") and the direction of the behavior (for example, "The comment should be relevant to the selected topic and substantive"). A student may "misbehave" by always offering questions and never giving opinions; by talking too much or not at all; by bringing up irrelevant material or offering a joke. If you are seeing widespread misbehavior, examine your instructions. It is probably not possible to write instructions that will never be misinterpreted, but you can reduce the odds of misinterpretation.

Schneider (1998) suggests including a section in your syllabus detailing appropriate classroom behavior. One function of this section is to instruct students, and it should be mentioned on the first day of class. Another function is to demonstrate to appeal committees, should a student ever complain, that you have clearly described appropriate behavior to students. A clear syllabus can be protection for you. Grunert (1997) provides suggestions for syllabus development.

What Did You Do? Did It Work? Objective evaluation of your efforts is critical for improvement and for effective follow-up. Asking for honest, critical reflection by a party not personally involved can help you generate alternatives. This reflection could be used in future similar circumstances to avoid or resolve problems more effectively. Classroom assessment techniques (Angelo and Cross, 1993) can help you to evaluate the effectiveness of some interventions.

Understanding the Reasons for Difficult Behavior

Asking why a behavior occurs is not typically as useful as popularly believed. It is usually sufficient to describe the behavior without inference, identify emotional responses, and appreciate the effect of the behavior's consequences. At times, however, understanding the variety of causes that could contribute to disruptive behavior in the classroom can help you select the most appropriate solution. Although the following list is not exhaustive, it should provide a reasonable sampling of explanations for problem behavior and may help the instructor respond more empathically and, thus, more calmly.

Physical Causes. Although the instructor does not necessarily have any control over the following contributions to uncivil behavior, understanding their impact can be helpful.

Medication, Drugs, and Other Substances. College students ingest legal, illegal, or tolerated substances that alter their behavior in myriad ways. It is naive to think the substance will be cleared from their systems before attending class. I (Layne) once took students on a tour of a mental hospital, and one student arrived drunk. Students whose behavior has gone to extremes (drowsy, overly active) from their typical behavior may be reacting to or recovering from some substance. Student tolerance for others' behavior may also be reduced by ingested substances.

Unfortunately, recall of learning is state dependent. Students are more likely to recall information when they are in the same state (drunk, for example) as when they learned it (Eich, 1909). (Of course, the overall level of learning is likely to be impaired by some states, so what the student recalls is less than she would remember if she had learned it while sober.)

Do not assume that all substance reactions are due to recreational drugs. Medication schedules may be disrupted due to the normal stresses of academic life. In turn, this could cause behavioral changes such as irritability or loss of ability to focus. These, then, may produce disruptive behavior. A diabetic student may not monitor his diet and appear drunk. Someone with a mild closed-head brain injury may have increasing difficulty focusing when stressed.

Illnesses. College students tend to be poor at taking care of their health. Those living in residence halls are exposed to many sources of illness. Feeling ill can make anyone irritable, although confusion and inattention may be more typical reactions. Students may also have life-threatening illnesses and could be coping with very serious health problems such as cancer or AIDS. Some chronic illnesses, such as diabetes, or chronic pain, perhaps from injuries or arthritis, can produce increased irritability. Some illnesses may result in sleep disruption, which can lead a student to fall asleep in class. I (Layne) had an excellent student with narcolepsy who occasionally fell asleep when her medication was not adjusted properly. Such a student may stop coming to class rather than confess a personal medical history to an instructor angry over her "misbehavior."

College students may suffer from any of a variety of mental illnesses, from depression to schizophrenia. In general, persons with mental illness are less dangerous than the rest of the population. Their behavior may be unusual but is not generally purposefully disruptive. They may, in fact, be at greater risk of being overlooked in the classroom because of their inhibitions.

One category of emotional problem does present special problems. Those who have personality disorders are by definition disruptive in their interpersonal relationships. In general students with these pervasive problems are among the most challenging to deal with, particularly because they appear at first to be typical students. With time, however, it becomes apparent that it is beyond the typical instructor's skills to manage their behavior. At that point, it may be advisable to refer a student to professional help. Characteristics of a personality disorder include always being in extreme crisis, interpreting innocent material in a paranoid manner, repeated deceitfulness (often combined with superficial charm), being inappropriately sexually seductive or interpersonally exploitative, or needing an excessive amount of advice to make decisions (American Psychiatric Association, 1994). You should not make a diagnosis from this list of characteristics, but it might give you an idea of the nature of personality disorder and why professional referral is necessary.

Fatigue. It is common in academic life for irritability to increase as exams approach. As time pressures increase, civility is often lost. Students may be working multiple jobs or night shifts in addition to studying. For some, "pulling an all-nighter" is almost a rite of passage, with attendant potential loss of alertness and interpersonal sensitivity. I (Kuhlenschmidt) had a student working close to a full-time job, taking a full course load, applying to graduate schools, and living with an infant son and a troubled nephew.

Discomfort. Classrooms that are too hot or cold, seats that are uncomfortable, or a class schedule that prevents a student from eating regularly can cause irritability, which may be expressed toward others. I (Layne) recently had a pregnant student whose severe nausea made it difficult for her to learn in class.

Vision and Hearing Problems. Mild visual or hearing disabilities may not be readily apparent to an observer. A student with such a disability may appear disruptive. This issue was made all too apparent to me (Kuhlenschmidt) when a student whom I had confronted for constant whispering volunteered that she was hard of hearing. Instead of punishing the student, I started handing out a printed outline of my class material. Unfortunately, recent generations of students are at particular risk for hearing loss from exposure to loud concerts and headphones. Large classrooms may be especially frustrating for these students. Vision or hearing problems (particularly unidentified ones) of either a student or the instructor increase the possibility of miscommunication and the likelihood that offense will be taken.

Emotional Challenges. An instructor has to decide whether to become personally involved when emotional challenges are the cause of uncivil behavior. Being empathetic in the face of distress or anger can defuse some situations. Talking confidentially with colleagues or the counseling center can help the instructor decide when a student needs referral for professional help.

Loss. College students have reached an age at which they are considered adult in our culture. As a result they are given increasing responsibility for major life decisions and they may feel isolated when faced with loss. Although some "grandmother deaths" are excuses, students do face some very real losses, including loss of the protection of childhood, loss of childhood home, and loss of loved ones. Grief may be expressed as anger or as high levels of activity as well as guilt, depression, withdrawal, and denial. When persons of any age feel a loss of control, they are likely to try to regain control by any means possible.

On occasion an entire class (including you) may need to deal with a loss (for example, the death of a classmate). You will need to inform the class of the facts surrounding the loss. The group will likely benefit from some class time to absorb the news. Those who might need to leave should be allowed to, but rather than dismissing the class, you should give them an opportunity to discuss the event and express their feelings. They may wish to memorialize the event or person (for example, by planting a tree), perhaps as a group. Students who wish to do so should be allowed to attend funeral services. Common emotional reactions are shock, numbness, guilt, and anger. There is no "right" way to grieve or a "correct" amount of grief. Grief will generally come in its own time. You may see signs of mourning through the remainder of the semester, including some disruption. Remember that you need to grieve also.

Maturity. College students on the cusp of adulthood still have much to learn about taking on adult responsibilities and balancing demands. Under stress, some students are likely to revert to childlike ways of coping, including strong emotional outbursts. Some individuals have a hard time stopping themselves once they begin to get upset. You may find yourself teaching these students how to behave and setting limits for them as if they were much younger.

Attention Seeking. Students who are lonely or feel isolated may have learned to obtain attention through disruptive behaviors. You may have some success by carefully attending to this type of student when the student is behaving appropriately and ignoring him when disruptive. As the student learns how to elicit appropriate attention, the disruptive behavior may be reduced.

Redirected Aggression. Students may be upset over some event unrelated or peripherally related to the class. A small event in the class (for example, forgetting the textbook) may trigger a disproportionately large response. The teacher is simply an available target for the expression of their emotion. A classroom debate may feed an already existing state of emotional arousal. It is easier for this student to blame a problem on someone else than to take personal responsibility. This is very common with regard to poor performance on course papers and exams and is expressed in phrases such as, "The teacher gave me an F." You might be tempted to point out that the student earns the grade, but that may not likely be convincing. If the student were emotionally ready to accept responsibility, then he or she would likely have done so without prompting.

Traditional college students face the developmental task of building identity (Erikson, 1968). They are learning the meaning of independence. We have been teaching them to be critical thinkers, and they have learned they can challenge authority. Students may feel safer challenging an instructor—a surrogate parent—than challenging their actual parents. In some sense, the student may be "practicing" on the instructor and on the college environment.

Environmental Factors. The instructor has more control over some of these elements, which can contribute to a positive classroom experience.

Norms for Conduct. The first day and the syllabus are very important for establishing expectations for appropriate and inappropriate behavior and for demonstrations of the seriousness of the rules. If you do not enforce and do not demonstrate the rules in the syllabus, then the students are less likely to obey them. As a rule of thumb, an instructor can get "easier" but not "harder" and still maintain order as the semester progresses.

Class Size. The size of the class will influence the norms established. Large classes may encourage students to act as if they were in a movie theater or watching television. You must be clear in your directions and in deliberate crowd control (by using seating charts, for example). Cooperative learning activities may help reduce the barriers that a large class erects between you and your students.

Culture. Varied values and customs concerning the appropriateness of classroom behaviors need to be addressed by the instructor, particularly in larger classrooms where there may be a highly diverse student body. Different cultures have different standards concerning lateness or when it is appropriate to speak, for example. Cultural differences may also occur across economic lines. You may need to be explicit regarding your expectations. If most of the students are going to work in a particular cultural environment following graduation, then it may be easier to justify classroom norms based on that work environment. On the other hand, students planning to return to different environments may place no value on learning "foreign" behaviors. (Chapter Seven, this volume, discusses the challenges of civility in a diverse classroom more fully.)

Task. If disruption revolves around an assigned task, examine the task elements. Vague or confusing instructions can lead to frustration, which may be displaced. Although the task may seem simple to the instructor, the student's ease or difficulty with the task should be the determining factor for simplicity. Global instructions are not fair if the instructor accepts only a narrow range of products. A take-home exam, for example, ought to have minimums and limits on the length and on the resources expected. Expecting too much, given the knowledge and skill level, may also result in frustration. Although a student may express anger toward you, it may be anger at self for being unable to complete a task. You could use this as an opportunity for teaching how to deal constructively with the inevitable frustrations that come in every field.

A larger issue deals with student motivation to complete the task, or even to take the course, particularly if it is a general education course. Some instructors resist using motivational techniques to increase student learning, asserting that students should arrive motivated. Although that may be true to some extent, neglecting motivational dimensions is likely to result in disruptive behavior. Teaching students subject matter usually includes teaching why the subject matter is important in the big picture. Helping students make that discovery for themselves can generate motivation and improve classroom behavior. Try asking students to write a paragraph describing why they think the course might be worthwhile. They could consider factors concerning their chosen major, their social life, or the type of life they want to be living in ten years. Having to generate and write down reasons helps them to make the reasons part of their way of thinking.

Routine and Stimulation. In general, too much routine produces boredom, but too little produces chaos. Too much stimulation creates problems for those who ordinarily have difficulty managing their activity level, and too little stimulation leads others to create stimulation, disrupting the class. You can moderate these tendencies by using some varying instructional methods during a class session and across a semester.

Modifying Instructor and Student Behavior

Students observe you and their classmates. They imitate behavior that generates acceptable responses. If you engage in uncivil behavior toward students, then students are more likely to behave similarly toward you or toward other students. Classmates who are uncivil without some immediate consequence from you become role models to other students, to the detriment of the class.

Conversely, rewarding desirable behavior sets the standard for appropriate behavior and creates a positive environment for learning. Unfortunately, it is easy to punish desired behavior accidentally. A student who offers a comment and is greeted with a criticism or sarcastic statement experiences an aggressive environment. You may not intend to sound or be sarcastic, but the power relationship and your greater knowledge and subsequent quickness to respond may have that effect. Asking instead for comments from other students in the class can help to depersonalize commentary.

Another challenge is to avoid rewarding undesirable behavior. An instructor who gives in to whining or to outbursts of temper is teaching students that uncivil behavior is acceptable. Ignoring clearly unacceptable behavior is also not desirable because students may interpret silence as assent.

If immediate action is necessary, you should ask the student to meet you after class or to step into the hall for a moment. The most desirable resolutions occur when both parties are calm. Delaying discussing the problem for a day may be necessary. When communicating to the student regarding disruptive behavior, use behavioral examples with no inferences. Do not label the person's behavior as "angry" or "out of control." Those are inferences and may be at odds with the student's personal experience. Secondary arguments about the nature of the problem are the result.

Focusing on what was observed is more effective. For example, say, "Three times you started speaking while I had the floor," rather than, "You are rude." State that the behavior is not acceptable and explain what the student needs to do (again a behavior, not an inference). You might say, for example, "I need you to raise your hand and wait for me to acknowledge you before speaking." A related but ineffective inference would be, "I need you to be more polite." "Politeness" is open to interpretation.

The circumstances should help you decide whether to give a reason that the behavior is not acceptable with your request. Giving reasons can lead to arguments over whether those are valid reasons. On the other hand, providing reasons can help achieve compliance. Just because you have stated a preference does not mean the person will necessarily engage in the behavior. Students are human beings, not puppets, and they will exercise freedom of choice. If the disruptive behavior continues, the teacher may need to speak with the department head or dean of student life about excluding the student from the class. For further help in being assertive, and not aggressive or passive, the book *Your Perfect Right* (Alberti and Emmons, 1990) may be a useful resource.

If a student is very inappropriate and disruptive (for example, shouting or being incoherent), it may be necessary to send a student to the departmental office for assistance. Do not take risks with the class or yourself. Do not meet behind closed doors alone with a student who is increasingly agitated. If the instructor and others remain calm but the student is not calming down, then professional intervention should be sought. Professional help may also be needed if the person seems illogical or the behavior is bizarre. Although this might seem like obvious advice, under the stress of an unusual situation, it is not easy to remember. A colleague reports that when he was a graduate student, a faculty member was found huddled under a desk, muttering and clearly incoherent. The frightened department chairman and our colleague drove the unwilling professor across several state lines to a relative's home. The risks the chairman took were enormous, for him, our graduate student colleague, and the disturbed professor. Periodically reviewing this material and at least mentally rehearsing the steps can help you be prepared to think of effective coping behavior when the occasion arises.

If time permits, it can be desirable to generate several plans for dealing with the problem behavior. When talking with the student, the teacher will have several options, depending on the information the student provides. Multiple plans allow the teacher to feel more in control. Select a realistic coping strategy. Once you have reviewed the various questions and possible explanations for problem behavior, you are ready to develop a list of options for dealing with the behavior. Although this problem-solving approach to disruptive classroom behavior may sound like a smooth progression, in real life the journey toward effective behavior management is a rocky road. You may need to try several approaches during a class. A solution that worked with one student may fail with another. Although a recipe for successful interpersonal relationships would be nice to have, the truth is that there are too many variables in any circumstance to achieve perfection. What you can do is increase the probability that you will find a solution by considering the variables and issues suggested here. Reflection and discussion with experienced instructors can be very important in improving your skill in this area. Interpersonal problem solving is partially a skill to be mastered and partially an art to be cultivated.

Some general characteristics apply across every strategy. Consistency in style is important because it gives students a predictable environment. (Some flexibility is desired to meet unexpected circumstances.) Attending to motivational elements can help your students buy into your course from the beginning, again reducing the chances of disruption. Finally, making an effort to connect with your students helps them to see you as a human being. Connecting also helps you to be attuned to their frustrations and upsets that lead to problem behavior.

Recognizing your limitations is part of that skill and art. Personal characteristics, such as being female, being small, having a soft voice, or being shy, may increase your challenges when dealing with disruptive behavior. Some characteristics cannot be changed, but there are instances of individuals who have demonstrated ability to manage disruptive behavior despite any of these personal characteristics. Perhaps you could identify someone sharing a quality and talk with that person about how he or she has learned to manage. My voice (Kuhlenschmidt) was very soft when I began teaching. I took a class on voice control and what was a regularly cited problem disappeared from my evaluations. Clothing selections and hair styles can undercut your authority or support it. You will be making a statement by how you appear. Whether it is the statement that is helpful to you as a teacher is your choice.

You cannot make students feel a particular emotion, but you can reassure students or attend to their emotional needs. You may not be successful in changing student behavior, but you can change yourself, your behavior, your feelings, and your expectations of coping with uncivil behavior. You can try to alter the environment or at least take action to prevent the problem from occurring again. You can remind everyone of the rules. You can change tasks or your syllabus. Sometimes you can redirect or rechannel student behavior or distract student attention. Most important you can support desirable behavior and help students in distress feel more worthwhile.

Conclusion

Carefully considering the questions and options in this chapter can help you to become more effective in dealing with disruptive student behavior. When selecting coping strategies, be realistic in what you can accomplish as an instructor. Take a moment, if you have not yet done so, and identify the available referral resources and institutional policies on your campus concerning disruptive behavior. Contact the dean of student life, the counseling center, and the security office. Having these tools readily available will help you effectively manage disruptive behavior in your classroom.

References

Alberti, R., and Emmons, M. *Your Perfect Right*. San Luis Obispo, Calif.: Impact, 1990.
American Psychiatric Association. *Diagnostic and Statistical Manual of Mental Disorders*. (4th ed.) Washington, D.C.: American Psychiatric Association, 1994.
Angelo, T., and Cross, K. *Classroom Assessment Techniques*. (2nd ed.) San Francisco: Jossey-Bass, 1993.
Eich, E. "Theoretical Issues in State Dependent Memory." In H. L. Roediger III and F.I.M. Carik (eds.), *Varieties of Memory and Consciousness*. Hillsdale, N.J.: Erlbaum, 1989.
Erikson, E. *Identity: Youth and Crisis*. New York: Norton, 1968.
Grunert, J. *The Course Syllabus*. Bolton, Mass.: Anker, 1997.
Schneider, A. "Insubordination and Intimidation Signal the End of Decorum in Many Classrooms." *Chronicle of Higher Education*, Mar. 27, 1998, pp. A12–A14.

SALLY L. KUHLENSCHMIDT is director of the Center for Teaching and Learning and associate professor of psychology at Western Kentucky University in Bowling Green, Kentucky.

LOIS E. LAYNE is professor of psychology at Western Kentucky University in Bowling Green, Kentucky.

To manage conflict effectively, faculty need to be able to understand and analyze the problem and possible solutions. Conflict management involves problem identification, solution identification, and solution implementation.

After the Eruption: Managing Conflict in the Classroom

Susan A Holton

Conflict has always been a part of the classroom. "In medieval times, students were forbidden to shout, hiss, make noise, throw stones in class or deputize one's servant to do so. In the 1300s the Bishop in the Episcopal Court of Parish said, 'They attend classes but make no effort to learn anything'" (Bishop, n.d., p. 72).

In early American classrooms, student uprisings were not uncommon. The Great Rebellion of 1823 at Harvard found students "drowning out tutors' voices in the classroom, drenching people with buckets of ink and water and more" (Cowley and Williams, 1991, p. 105). At Yale in the 1840s, students "were wont to express their displeasure with their tutors by stoning their windows and attacking them with clubs if they chanced out after dark" (Fulton and Thompson, 1991, p. 9).

Conflict has accompanied academia throughout its history. In the 1960s and 1970s conflict rose in the American classroom as college students often angrily demanded relevance, respect, and a voice.

Although we rarely dodge stones in the classroom, and I have yet to have a servant deputized by one of my students for purposes of harassing me, conflict is a fact in the American classroom. The range of classroom incivilities go from mild inattention to physical violence. Although the majority of the classroom conflict is on the nonviolent continuum, that does not mean that it is nondisruptive. Mild conflict is obviously easier to handle.

On my syllabus I state clearly that students may not wear baseball caps to class. When students walk in on the first day, I ask anyone with a cap to remove it. When we review the syllabus together, I point out my policy. At the end of the syllabus review, I ask if there are any questions, and I invariably answer the "no hats" question. The next period when someone comes in with a hat, I merely privately and gently remind the person of the policy.

Much of mild conflict can be handled in that way. By including your own rules in the syllabus, you make students aware of your classroom expectations, perhaps also including the consequences for failing to meet those expectations. For example, you may write that recurrent lateness or repeated absences will result in a lowered grade. As Sally Kuhlenschmidt noted in Chapter Two (this volume), the student has a choice of the way he or she will react. But you have been clear about your expectations.

At the other end of the spectrum is extreme physical violence. If that should occur in the classroom, there must be immediate action, including the possibility of expulsion of the offender. Campus security should be called immediately, and the student should not be allowed to return to class.

Much of the conflict on campus falls between these two ends of the continuum. The types of conflict that I focus on in this chapter could be characterized as serious, open arguments between faculty and students or between students themselves.

There is a plethora of tactics to use to avoid conflict and create classroom communities where students feel valued and engaged, but when the conflict occurs, it must be managed. If it is not dealt with, the other students may assume that the behavior is tolerable. Other students will begin to have side conversations, read the newspaper, listen to their music, get up and leave, or worse.

It is also necessary for professors to manage conflict effectively because whatever they do will come back to haunt them. The student grapevine works rapidly and lets all students know what they can get away with in a classroom. Most professors have war stories about conflicts that were managed unsuccessfully and have brilliant ideas, in retrospect, about what should have been done.

The process that I suggest to manage conflict in the classroom can take from an hour to weeks or longer, depending on the nature and the severity of the conflict. It is well worth the investment of time. Only after investing the time will you understand the *real* problem behind the conflictual behavior and be able to manage, rather than put a Band-Aid on, the behavior. And the conflict you understand and manage effectively will not come back to haunt you.

The Holton Model for Conflict Management (Holton, 1998) has three parts: (1) problem identification, (2) solution identification, and (3) solution implementation. All three steps are necessary; to leave one out means that the conflict will not be adequately analyzed, understood, and managed.

My student teaching was in an idyllic setting. Miami University inaugurated a "student teaching overseas" program during my senior year, and because I was working in the Office of International Students, I learned about it. I applied to go to Athens, Greece, and so found myself in a class of high school juniors and seniors studying English. When I finally got to teach, I discovered that some students were talking to each other throughout the class period. I was devastated! They were supposed to be listening to my newly minted pearls of wisdom.

But I thought to ask some questions before I sent everyone to detention. I discovered that the students in question were new to the school and to the English language. Despite a rule requiring each student to be fluent in English, it was clear that many of these children of embassy families were not. And so much translating went on during classes. They were not whispering about their weekend plans. They were translating my words to their peers.

In order to manage any classroom conflict effectively, we have to understand what it is. That requires that the professor step back and gather information before acting. Otherwise you may be addressing the wrong problem, embarrassing yourself or the student, or inflicting more harm than good.

Too often professors, like others, make attempts to manage a conflict before gathering all of the information. When these attempts fail, participants are surprised to learn that they forgot to determine one of the pieces of the conflict puzzle. A wise professor knows that the problem well defined is half solved; the same is true for the conflict well defined.

Problem Identification

The identification phase requires six steps, each necessary to understand the conflict.

Who Is Involved? If a single person or a small group of people are involved in the disruptive behavior, you can address that specific group or individual. The problem may be contained within that group. If it is more diffuse, then that is important information as well.

It is important to identify all of the parties who are involved in the conflict—and all who are not (this may be just as important as you try to understand the conflict). If the players in the conflict keep changing, that is also important to know. You will need to gather information from everyone involved in the conflict, and so you must identify those people.

You also should manage the conflict with the smallest group possible. If three people are regularly disrupting the class with inappropriate statements, you need to deal with those three people, not the entire class. If you let the conflict continue, though, it may spread to the whole class. If you can identify and analyze the conflict early in its life, then you can keep it restricted. Think of the conflict like a forest fire. The best course of action is to douse the match right away; if you cannot or do not, the fire will spread. The sooner you put it out, the better off you are, and the fewer people will be burned.

Identify the relationship between the people in conflict. Is the conflict between two students, a student and a graduate student, a student and you, or a student and another professor in the department? (If the last is the case, the student is taking it out on you.) Are the people in conflict roommates? Former lovers now in a tumultuous breakup? Rivals for the lead in the next play? The relationship of those in conflict is important to understanding the conflict and developing solutions. A conflict between a faculty member and a student is very different from that of two colleagues. The power relationship in conflict cannot be ignored.

It is also important to determine the people who are peripheral to the conflict but likely to be affected by it if it is not managed or escalates. In classroom conflict, everyone in the room is peripherally involved; if the conflict is not effectively managed, it is going to affect the classroom climate and the learning of the rest of the class. A conflict poorly understood and managed also can have negative consequences for the entire department.

Are there ghosts operating in this conflict situation? Does the sight of the rugby team members huddled together in the back of the room remind you of a group with whom you had problems last year? You may expect problems again and react in a biased way. Or perhaps two years ago you had a single father who always missed class during his children's school vacations. You are ready for this new one, and have your arguments and anger set to go before this semester's single parent even broaches the subject. Beware of the ghosts.

What Is the Conflict? In determining the "what," it is important to identify both the emotional and objective facts. Too often people trying to understand and manage conflict ignore the emotional aspects—at their peril. If they are ignored, they will come back to affect the conflict and attempts at management. And everyone will wonder why the conflict returns . . . and returns . . . and returns. It will return if you are identifying and acknowledging only one part of the conflict.

If you are working with a group of students to understand why they are constantly fighting with you, objecting to every assignment, and complaining loudly about what you are teaching, you may find that they already had a lot of the material in a previous class. That is objective fact. You may also find that they feel frustrated that the information is being repeated and that their time is being wasted. They may feel that you are not honoring their knowledge and abilities by making this repetition. Those are the emotional facts.

When Did It Happen? The longer a conflict goes on, the more difficult it is to determine when it began. If you work with the conflict immediately, you can tell the "when." You can stop the students immediately after class and say, "When you talked to each other throughout most of today's class, I was quite annoyed. It made it difficult for me to concentrate on my material, and I feel that I did not teach the concepts as well as I wanted to."

If you address the students immediately, they will remember the incident. If you wait until the next class period or later, the students are likely to forget it (or to say that they forgot). And if you do not express your displeasure until the next class meeting, they are very likely to repeat the behavior—and irritate you even more!

If you let the conflict go on, the beginning will be more difficult to pin down. It will be difficult to define the problem or to remember the initiating circumstance. So it is important to identify the origins, or as close as you can get to the original incident(s) of the conflict.

It also helps to determine whether it is an ongoing or cyclical conflict. During registration every semester, for example, conflicts occur because students are caught between their desire to do well in current classes and the need to register for next semester's classes. They make choices that are not always the ones a professor would encourage. In order to get in line early enough to register for a limited number of classes, a student may miss a test and then have a conflict with her professor about making it up. Knowing that the seasonal conflict will occur again allows us to work with the student records office to manage the conflict before it even takes place. Perhaps conflicts in class occur at the end of every semester when everyone, students and professors, is stressed. Perhaps conflicts occur at the beginning of the semester when you have not yet established your rules (although those should be established the first minute the group gets together). It is important to identify when a conflict occurs.

Where Did It Happen? Does conflict occur more often in the large lecture than in your small classes? That may tell you that you need to work on your skills in teaching large lecture classes. Does it occur only in one room and not in others? That may tell you something about the space. Are your students always late in one particular class? Might there be a physical reason for that? It is important to know not only where the conflict occurred physically (in the classroom, in the office), but also where within the organizational structure. Does conflict occur between teaching assistants and students, but rarely between senior faculty and the same students? Or does conflict always occur between two groups of students in class? The management possibilities may be different if it was between peers or between a student and a graduate teaching assistant.

Resolution Attempts. What have you already tried? What have others working with the same students tried? Perhaps in your institution there is a problem with a certain group of students. The members of the most popular sorority on campus always sit in the back of the room, challenge you on every assignment, and answer every question sarcastically. Do they react in the same way in other classes? If they do, that will give you some information about that group of people, and you may want to work with colleagues to manage the conflicts. What have others done to manage the conflict that occurs when members of the baseball team leave before exams so that they can play in their tournament?

In order to understand a conflict, you must know what attempts have been made to manage the conflict and whether those attempts have been successful in any way. If they have been successful, you may want to adopt the same methods. If they have not, you will want to avoid them and come up with alternatives.

Consequences of the Conflict. It is important to think through the consequences of a conflict and of any conflict management style that you use. The consequences will vary with each classroom situation. And you have to decide whether your best course of action is to let the behavior go, thus avoiding the conflict, or whether to manage it actively in some way, either immediately or after a delay.

I had to do a quick conflict analysis when I was confronted by a student who got up and left my lecture class of two hundred students barely halfway through the class period. I had to think quickly about my options. If I had confronted him publicly, asking where he was going, then I would have succeeded in embarrassing him, calling attention to him (something he might have been seeking by his action). I would have been taking more attention from the content and refocusing the students' attention. Those who did not see him leave would now have looked at him, wondered what was happening, and lost their thought patterns. So I let it go. If he leaves every week, I will confront him about it privately at the beginning of class. When I did that last week, he assured me that he was going to stay this week, and other weeks. He did stay last week; I will see if he continues to do so.

What will happen if I let the sorority members continue their behavior? It will probably grow worse, I certainly will get angrier, and the conflict will escalate. With that group I need to do some conflict management.

Completing the Problem Identification Stage. After you have completed the problem identification stage, you will be able to define the problem. Sometimes at this stage you determine that the conflict is manageable only by expelling the student from the class. Although most of us are reluctant to do that, it is a conflict management style that is open to use and should be used. Most often, however, you and the students involved in the conflict can work together, sometimes with the aid of a third party—for example, from the department, from student services, or an outside third party—to identify solutions to your conflict.

In this stage you also identified the players in the conflict situation. All of those directly involved in the conflict must work together to identify solutions. If you leave someone out of the next two stages, the conflict management process that the rest of you agree on may be easily sabotaged.

Solution Identification

The development of solutions is not a simple process. Setting the stage and getting parties to communicate and work together are necessary parts of this phase of the process. This second phase of conflict management must not be shortened. Often marvelous options for management are ignored out of the intense drive for conclusion.

Develop a Positive Attitude. No conflict will be managed by people who are sure it is doomed to failure or refuse to sit in the same room with the other parties. Everyone who is involved in the conflict must agree to work together and acknowledge that some sort of agreement is possible that will be acceptable to everyone. This may require a discussion about ways in which they might benefit from working together in the future and about the positive outcomes that are possible as a result of the management of this conflict.

Establish Ground Rules. Conflict often produces a feeling of chaos. In order to ameliorate that feeling, it is important to establish ground rules for the group's work. The ground rules should cover structure (when, where, how often, how long we will meet), communication (speaking for oneself, using "I" statements, confidentiality), and parties (who will be involved). It is also necessary to get a verbal commitment from everyone to stay with the process until it is concluded.

Identify Interests of the Parties. What do the people in the conflict want? If a student refuses to work with other students in a group project, I need to understand why. I may discover that she is not just being obstinate, but that the rest of the group can meet only on weekends and the student in question has a job.

Roger Fisher and William Ury have written extensively about the importance of interests versus positions in their book *Getting to Yes* (1981) and in subsequent books by each author. They say that parties need to understand what each one truly wants.

At the beginning of my research methodology class, I have students write research papers about their names. I want them to learn how to find sources and how to write an objective paper. I also think that it is fun for them to learn this information about themselves.

Suppose I have a student who declares vociferously that she will not fulfill my assignment. I need to understand why. If I merely hear that she does not want to write the paper, which of course I have thought out and know is the best way to learn the concepts, I am likely to be offended and not want to budge. What we then get is two immovable objects. Instead of merely butting heads over the assignment, we both need to answer "Why?" Why do I want her to write a paper on the origins of her name? And why doesn't she want to do that? When we ask why each of us feels the way we do, she discovers that my intent is to have her learn basic research skills in a way that I think will be personally interesting and to learn how to write an objective paper. She explains to me that she is adopted (but did not want to reveal that in class) and she does not want to write about it in a paper or delve into it in any way. After we understand the "whys" we can quit butting heads and together work on a way to manage our conflict.

As the people involved in a conflict identify interests rather than hold to their immovable positions, the conflict changes shape and becomes manageable.

Develop Alternatives. There is never only one way to manage a conflict, one solution to a problem. But often in the middle of conflict, it is difficult to see options. This phase therefore is very important.

Brainstorming is the best process to develop alternatives. In an environment of trust (sometimes facilitated by the neutral third party) disputants can work together to develop multiple alternatives. Sometimes it is helpful to have others, not just the parties involved in the conflict, join in this brainstorming stage. If the trust level is high enough, you may involve other students and faculty, who will identify some options that you may not be able to see.

It is also helpful to identify ways that similar issues have been managed by others. How have other faculty and students resolved similar issues? What has been done at other institutions? Knowledge of solutions that others have used gives the disputants not necessarily the right answer but an acknowledgment that solutions are possible, and may expand their concepts of possible alternatives.

It is important that this phase be separate from decision making based on criteria.

Identify Criteria. If you have done brainstorming well, you will have some potential solutions that are inappropriate for a variety of reasons and even some that are illegal or ridiculous. It is then necessary to identify appropriate criteria and to use those criteria to determine the "best" solutions.

Given the nature of the conflict, there will probably be some objective criteria. The student may have to finish a final project, but perhaps the nature of that project could be negotiated. The student must behave appropriately in class but wants some outlet for her frustration. Some criteria are also subjective. These are often overlooked, to the detriment of the conflict management process. But emotions are important factors in conflict management, and so one criterion may be that all parties feel good about the solution.

In the situation with the adopted student and the name paper, I would not be willing to forgo the assignment. I want her to have a relatively painless and fun way to learn how to do research. But since my chosen topic is neither painless nor fun for her, together we can brainstorm and decide on a topic that would be interesting for her and fulfill my requirements.

Weigh Solutions Against Criteria. After the criteria are identified, the brainstormed solutions should be weighed against them. The end result should be the "best" solution to the conflict. It is important to determine whether that solution is, in fact, felt to be the "best" by all parties. If you have used the criteria against each idea and the "best" does not feel like a good solution, it means that you left out some important criteria. Commonly the criteria left out are the subjective ones.

The conflict has been identified and the solutions have been identified, so you think you must be finished. You are not. The implementation phase needs to be done with as much care and time as the other two. Again, rushing this third step is done only at the risk of jeopardizing the conflict management process and failing to satisfy the people involved.

Solution Implementation

Every one of us has agreed to a solution to a problem, walked away, and wondered why nothing happened. Unless you pay attention to this phase of the conflict management process, all of the work you have done will be lost.

Develop a Plan of Action. It is necessary to be detailed and specific in your plan of action. Failure to be specific will result in differing perceptions of the solution and a failure of the conflict management process. In this phase the plan of action should address a number of issues.

Who is going to be involved in the implementation of the solutions? This will include the parties who have worked together to manage this conflict, but it also may include others. In the example of the disruptive sorority sisters, this step will certainly include the members in class and me. It also would likely include the adviser for the sorority, perhaps the student activities director, and perhaps some other members of the sorority. It is important to be specific about everyone who will be brought into the plan. Often it is important to include the department chair or the dean on this list because they need to be aware of the agreed solution.

What exactly is to be done? Nothing is too minor to be included on this list. If I am going to talk with the reference librarian to ask her to help a student find some resources, that meeting should be written down. If I am going to talk with the sorority adviser, that meeting too should be included. If it is not written down and included in the plan, it will be forgotten. And in a month, everyone will wonder what happened.

When are the parties going to act? What am I going to do tomorrow? What is the student deadline? In an agreement with a student who repeatedly fails to turn in papers, you might identify specific dates and times each week when he would turn in his work. In that way neither of you could question whether his work was on time or late. By what date will the complete solution be in place? That date may be at the end of the semester, or it may be tomorrow. Not all solutions have extended deadlines. There should be check-in dates when the parties meet to talk about the solution and the progress, and work with any issues that arise.

Who is responsible for mediating any differences between the parties? If, despite our good intentions, the plan does not work, who are we going to call in to mediate and help us? Can either one of us call in a third party if we feel that the process is not working?

This plan of action should be written up and signed by all parties, including any neutral third party. This document will be more valuable if every aspect of the agreement is clearly spelled out, and in terms that will not be debatable in the future.

Determine How to Handle Conflict in the Future. You have just successfully managed conflict. For you and the students involved, the process should serve as an educational experience. What worked about this? What did not work? How will you work (with either this student or with others) to manage any conflict that might occur in the future? As a part of the conflict management process, the parties should agree on a way to deal with further conflict. They may, for example, agree to go to the university ombudsperson, to appoint a conflict management committee, or to meet monthly to discuss issues and try to avert problems.

There will always be conflict in the classroom. The earliest recorded classrooms had it, and the one you worked with yesterday did as well. When we know how to analyze the problems, identify solutions, and develop ways to implement those solutions, then we can effectively manage any conflict that may occur in the classroom or beyond.

References

Bishop, M. "Scholares Medii Aevi." *Horizon,* n.d., pp. 66–79.
Cowley, W. H., and Williams, D. (eds.). *International and Historical Roots of American Higher Education.* New York: Garland, 1991.
Fisher, R., and Ury, W. *Getting to Yes: Negotiating Agreement Without Giving In.* Boston: Houghton Mifflin, 1981.
Fulton, J. F., and Thompson, E. "Benjamin Silliman." In W. H. Cowley and D. Williams (eds.), *International and Historical Roots of American Higher Education.* New York: Garland, 1991.
Holton, S. A. "Academic Mortar to Mend the Cracks: The Holton Model for Conflict Management." In S. A Holton (ed.), *Mending the Cracks in the Ivory Tower.* Bolton, Mass.: Anker, 1996.

SUSAN A HOLTON is professor of communication studies at Bridgewater State College in Bridgewater, Massachusetts. She is a consultant to educational and other organizations on issues of organizational conflict, change, and organizational dynamics.

This chapter examines issues associated with the classroom climate for a diverse student body and the role that faculty and students play in maintaining a tension-free, democratic, and effective learning environment.

Faculty Responsibility for Promoting Conflict-Free College Classrooms

James A. Anderson

Institutions of higher learning have as their primary mission the promotion of student learning and, ultimately, student success. More than any other group, college instructors are charged with executing this mission. Among the challenges that instructors face today is a new breed of students who, in many cases, approach the college classroom as a simulation of their real-world experience. They are often portrayed as members of the self-centered Generation X, no longer exhibiting the work ethic and the motive to achieve that historically has been attributed to college students.

Even more significant is the challenge generated by the diversity of the student body. They represent broad demographic categories and exhibit variations in cognitive skills, learning styles, communication patterns, motivational styles, and psychological characteristics. Such variations existed within the homogeneous population of traditional college students, but there is even greater variability in classrooms as the student body has become more diverse.

At the most fundamental level a college classroom can be thought of as a social arrangement among a diverse group of participants. At the center of this scenario is an instructor who may possess a high degree of expertise in an academic discipline but may not be as skilled at promoting an effective alliance among learners or between learners and himself or herself. Tiberius and Billson (1991) identify five key features underlying the alliance: (1) mutual respect, (2) shared responsibility for learning and mutual commitment to goals, (3) effective communication and feedback, (4) cooperation and willingness to negotiate conflicts, and (5) a sense of security in the classroom (see also Chapter One, this volume).

NEW DIRECTIONS FOR TEACHING AND LEARNING, no. 77, Spring 1999 © Jossey-Bass Publishers

Most faculty are not prepared to promote effective alliances within the classroom, primarily because their academic training gave them little opportunity to develop expertise in this area. Thus, they are often left to reconstruct the ideal learning environments that they remember from their own past, or, in the case of many part-time faculty, they attempt to transfer the mechanics of the professional workplace to the traditional classroom.

The instructor-student alliance relies on modes of effective communication between students, between students and instructors, and within the teaching-learning paradigm. Several authors have focused on the specific communication patterns that develop between instructors and students. Within that body of research literature, the concept of immediacy addresses the importance of communication that fosters closeness between people. Anderson (1979) found that immediacy positively influenced student attitudes toward teacher communication, course content, the course in general, and the course instructor. McCroskey and Richmond (1992) connect the concept of immediacy to the bases of power in a college classroom. In their summary of the research, they conclude that teacher immediacy results in increased student affect (affinity) for the teacher, increased student affect for the subject matter, increased student motivation, and, most important, reduced student resistance to teachers' attempts to influence their behavior. Immediate teachers have both more referent power and more actual power to manipulate classroom dynamics than do distant, noninvolved teachers.

Sanders and Wiseman (1994) suggest that immediacy is clearly linked to teaching effectiveness, especially with racially and culturally diverse student populations. Their study found that teacher immediacy behaviors enhance students' perceived cognitive, affective, and behavioral learning in the multicultural classroom. Some immediacy cues appear to have pancultural effects, while others hold particular salience for only certain ethnicities.

How do students make decisions about the nature of the social arrangement, and what do they bring to the classroom milieu that either facilitates or inhibits the teaching and learning process? Students observe and interpret the actions and cues (verbal and nonverbal) of the instructor and of other students. Many instructors tacitly assume that when college students enter a classroom, they are aware of their responsibility for learning and of the standards of civility that should be operative. The reality is that students come to college with disparate values, perceptions, and skills, representing their different demographic categories. The behavioral standards that students exhibit in the classroom to some degree are extensions of their standards outside it.

It would be naive to expect that the cultural values, behaviors, and expectations of diverse groups of students are so diluted on campus that their presence does not have an impact on classroom dynamics and learning outcomes. Students who enter a college classroom bring characteristics of the dominant campus culture and the persistent influence of their many parent cultures. Both of these help to shape the students' response to the learning environment and process. It is imperative that instructors recognize the potential bipolar impact of the presence of diversity in the classroom: the richness of diversity can elevate the learning process for all students when it is harnessed effectively, but it can become a source of classroom conflict when it is ignored or allowed to become a divisive force.

The opportunity for disruption in the college classroom is directly related to students' perception of their treatment by the instructor and other students, their sense of security, their perception of the classroom as a comfort zone, and the quality of the interpersonal rapport that exists. Lowman (1994) presents an interesting typology that compares the level of interpersonal rapport in a classroom with the effectiveness of instruction and the resultant impact on students. When that rapport is very low, relationships are deemed to be cold, distant, highly controlling, and unpredictable. Moreover, the instructor shows little interest in the students as persons and may be sarcastic or act openly disdainful toward them. Most significant is the fact that under these conditions, students begin to exhibit low motivation to learn, feel uneasy in class or around the teacher, and may experience significant anxiety or anger. Such conditions suggest the interaction of multiple factors that could serve to predict classroom incidents that disrupt or harm.

Classroom Climate and Faculty Responsibility

The research on student-professor interactions indicates that professors tend to hold differing expectations for students based on prior achievement, physical attractiveness, gender, socioeconomic status, and race and ethnicity. These differing expectations of students lead to differential treatment in the classroom (Jenkins and Bainer, 1994), which becomes more exaggerated as student learners become more diverse. Hall (1982) discusses the patterns of interruption that women and minorities experience in the classroom. Anderson (1988) and Brown (1986) cite the impact of culture and race on student learning and classroom interactions. Anderson and Adams (1992) focus on a conceptual paradigm that links diversity to classroom instruction.

This body of research as a whole suggests that diverse learners can be victimized by inequities in the college classroom. This victimization can affect academic performance, relations with majority students and with one another, academic and personal self-esteem, and the overall climate for learning. The quality of classroom teaching in theory is linked to the quality of interaction and to immediacy, so it is important for instructors to understand and direct student-teacher and student-student interactions. Instructors must begin to see the classroom as a social milieu replete with varied potentials for success and failure and for tension and cohesiveness.

As a social arrangement, the college classroom must appear safe and coercion free in order to produce optimal participation and minimal disruption. Instructors are responsible for identifying the appropriate rules, norms, and protocols that guarantee or at least maximize the chance that all students can become equal participants in the learning process.

Goodman (1995) discusses a framework for college classrooms that are diverse and where the potential for difficult dialogues therefore is pronounced. She suggests that teachers should use a model of social identity development that explores each individual's way of viewing the world and himself or herself as a member of a social group. This model is appropriate for both underrepresented and advantaged groups, and it helps students and the instructor to make sense of different reactions and perspectives. The five developmental stages of this model are naiveté, acceptance, resistance, redefinition, and internalization. In the classroom people tend to align with others at a similar stage. Tensions develop between and among students or students and the instructor at different points in the process because students believe that there is something at stake. For example, during the stage of resistance students may feel pressed to defend their own culture or cultural perspective against other students'. The cognitive dissonance that results from a clash of bipolar perspectives between students can initiate tension and can, if it is not resolved, sustain conflict. Student self-esteem can be threatened if the college classroom is seen as a competitive arena that lacks equity.

Establishing a Classroom Climate of Egalitarianism and Tolerance

Many instructors assume that students respect the differences they confront in the classroom and that they tolerate learning styles and worldviews that differ from theirs. This is not always so. Instructors and students share a responsibility to ensure that differences do not become a catalyst for inequality, harm, and dissension. Tiberius and Billson (1991) suggest several ways that this responsibility can be shared:

- Set the tone for openness and mutual responsibility early.
- Acknowledge feelings about differences and create a safe climate for discussion.
- Do not insist on a "politically correct" position; rather, help students explore all sides of a position.
- Do not allow inappropriate or harmful comments to pass unnoticed; instead explore the sources of such verbalizations and capitalize on teachable moments.

College teachers generally do not consider classroom behaviors that promote tension, lack civility, or cause social discomfort to be as disruptive or as harmful as those that intimidate, harass, or threaten. Hence, whether generated by a student or instructor, those behaviors that are viewed as less harmful are dealt with categorically in ways that are different from more serious ones. This is not to suggest that less harmful behaviors should be tolerated. If male athletes or fraternity members make sexist, racist, or homophobic comments in the classroom, their behavior should not be viewed simply as obnoxious boyish behavior. If an instructor intimidates or disparages a student or student group in the context of teaching, it can neither be excused nor protected under the umbrella of academic freedom.

Less harmful behaviors in the classroom exist and are tolerated because they are not deemed to be extreme, do not violate student codes of conduct, and do not transgress academic policy. They are often protected by the First Amendment right to free speech. The cumulative effect of such behaviors, however, takes a toll on students, especially those from diverse populations, as they expend energy to cope with them. Thus, less energy is available to facilitate their cognitive growth, selective attention, and positive learning outcomes. Teachers may respond in several ways, including one or more of the following: mediation, educational activities, training, and organizing.

Mediation. A dean or department chair is often charged with the task of establishing the protocol to guide mediation activities. Other people may be asked to participate if circumstances suggest that is necessary. For example, if the classroom conflict involves students of color as the victims or the initiators, a faculty or staff person of color may be asked to get involved. He or she could play the role of arbitrator or devil's advocate. The faculty or staff person could also lend emotional support, assist with the development of coping strategies, or represent the dean or department chair when necessary.

Mediation is often a stage development process, moving from informal or less formal levels to more formal ones. The level of effectiveness can vary depending on the training and background of the mediator(s), the clarity of the process to all parties, the motivation to resolve the conflict, and the availability of viable alternatives. (The mediation process is also considered in Chapters One, Six, Eight, and Nine in this volume.)

Educational Activities. This category of instructor response builds on activities that may already exist in the campus community, or new ones may be created. Although on the surface campuswide activities may seem to have a significant impact on tension and discomfort, they generally produce short-term results unless they are connected to more fundamental and recurring activities associated with classroom outcomes and their evaluation. Despite the energy they expend on large-scale events, most institutions respond to conflicts in the classroom in a reactive way, as isolated incidents, as opposed to developing a proactive and well-developed plan. Those who design and promote faculty development efforts should capitalize on the opportunity to strengthen faculty expertise in this area.

Useful campuswide educational activities commonly include the following:

- Discussions between groups involved in tense situations, or more general small group discussions at other times.
- Open forums, if tension or conflict has escalated and become public. Such forums can set the stage for the development of policies and practices on classroom civility.

- Workshops that seek to increase awareness and sensitivity and to foster intergroup tolerance.
- Residence life programs and counseling sessions for specific groups like fraternities, sororities, and athletes.
- Creation of liaison networks and web sites that allow for a broader sharing of information.
- A more visible administrative presence relative to these activities.

Significantly absent among these common educational responses is any recognition that the tension and conflict occur in an academic setting (the classroom) during an academic activity or process, yet the responses tend to reflect nonacademic and administrative origins. The normal academic process generally offers a myopic inclusion of tools and strategies to resolve classroom conflict and tension. This critical point needs to be pursued more extensively in addressing faculty responses to classroom difficulties.

Training. Although educational activities can serve as valuable tools in the mollification of classroom conflict and differences, they are not as goal oriented or outcome based as formal training efforts. Training can produce cadres of individuals across different levels of the institution who have the expertise to serve as quick-strike "SWAT teams" or who can guide long-term activities like formal committee work. For example, few faculty are aware of the well-documented teaching strategies that promote an equitable learning environment in the classroom. In such equitable classroom settings, incidents of tension and discomfort are minimized. Any institution could incorporate any of the following faculty development training activities as a hedge against potential classroom conflict:

- Orientation workshops for faculty, staff, and students that serve as a lead-in to future training
- University- or college-sponsored formal dialogues on diversity, differences, and multiculturalism
- Faculty development training on effective classroom dynamics
- Incentives for faculty who become involved in training activities

Organizing. It is important that any activities that address classroom climate be seen as well organized and directed toward substantive outcomes. The existence of policies, practices, and organizations suggests a higher level of commitment by an institution and increases the likelihood for success outcomes. Colleges and universities have a chance a priori to mitigate the occurrence of classroom conflicts by periodically engaging in introspective analyses of their policies and practices. Are the public statements about equity and diversity really operationalized and implemented in the arena most removed from public scrutiny: the college classroom? Does the institutional leadership assert itself in a proactive manner to marshal the institutional will and resources toward the development of an equitable climate for learning, especially for men and women

of color? Are all members of the institutional community aware of the consequences for uncivil and harmful behaviors and activities?

Useful organizing activities include the following:

- Organized meetings of key faculty, staff, and students to discuss classroom
  conflict and tension and to target outcomes
- Adoption of new policies and procedures on ways to prevent and address
  classroom conflict
- Creation of new organizations like a classroom climate committee with significant faculty representation

Some faculty may be concerned if administrators or the campus community try to legislate policies or practices on classroom behavior. It would be
more acceptable if existing processes that faculty value became the platform
for faculty development in this area. Although many colleges ask general committees or senior administrators to generate recommendations about dealing
with inappropriate or harmful classroom behavior, effective feedback should
most likely emerge instead from a faculty senate, a college committee, or a
department-based committee. It would also be valuable to try to incorporate
faculty roles and responsibility concerning inappropriate classroom behavior
into existing processes for faculty governance and grievances.

Conclusion

Although many college instructors feel unprepared to manage disruptive or
harmful behaviors in the college classroom, it is imperative that they receive
some training and feedback on how to negotiate difficult dialogues. Especially
as more students of color enter our institutions, we must offer an adequate
minimum guarantee of trust and security in the classroom.

Equity in the college classroom suggests that we introduce students to the
parameters of the conditions of effective learning, reduce the status differential between teacher and student and between students, and alert students to
their responsibility to one another.

References

Anderson, J. A. "Cognitive Styles and Multicultural Populations." *Journal of Teacher Education,* 1988, *39* (1), 2–9.

Anderson, J. A., and Adams, M. "Acknowledging Learning Styles of Diverse Populations:
Implications for the College Classroom." In L. Border and N. Chism (eds.), *Teaching for
Diversity.* New Directions for Teaching and Learning, no. 49. San Francisco: Jossey-Bass,
1992.

Anderson, J. F. "Teacher Immediacy as a Predictor of Teaching Effectiveness." In D. Nimmo
(ed.), *Communication Yearbook 3.* New Brunswick, N.J.: Transaction, 1979.

Brown, T. J. *Teaching Minorities More Effectively: A Model for Educators.* New York: University Press of America, 1986.

Goodman, D. "Difficult Dialogues: Enhancing Discussions About Diversity." *College Teaching*, 1995, *43* (2), 47–52.

Hall, R. M. *The Classroom Climate: A Chilly One for Women?* Project on the Status and Education of Women. Washington, D.C.: Association of American Colleges, 1982.

Jenkins, C. A., and Bainer, D. L. "Common Instructional Problems in the Multicultural Classroom." In K. A. Feldman and M. B. Paulsen (eds.), *Teaching and Learning in the College Classroom*. New York: Ginn Press, 1994.

Lowman, J. "What Constitutes Masterful Teaching." In K. A. Feldman and M. B. Paulsen (eds.), *Teaching and Learning in the College Classroom*. New York: Ginn Press, 1994.

McCroskey, J. C., and Richmond, V. P. "Increasing Teacher Influence Through Immediacy." In V. P. Richmond and J. C. McCroskey (eds.), *Power in the Classroom: Communication, Control, and Concern*. Hillsdale, N.J.: Erlbaum, 1992.

Sanders, J. A., and Wiseman, R. L. "The Effects of Verbal and Nonverbal Teacher Immediacy on Perceived Cognitive, Affective, and Behavioral Learning in the Multicultural Classroom." In K. Feldman and M. B. Paulsen (ed.), *Teaching and Learning in the College Classroom*. New York: Ginn Press, 1994.

Tiberius, R. G., and Billson, J. M. "The Social Context of Teaching and Learning." In R. J. Menges and M. D. Svinicki (eds.), *College Teaching: From Theory to Practice*. New Directions for Teaching and Learning, no. 45. San Francisco: Jossey-Bass, 1991.

JAMES A. ANDERSON is vice provost and dean of undergraduate studies at North Carolina State University.

By helping faculty collaborate to enrich their teaching abilities and by supporting them when faculty-student relationships fail occasionally, the department chair models leadership skills that faculty themselves can use.

Civility, Leadership, and the Classroom

Steven M. Richardson

College teachers work under a self-imposed handicap. Their responsibility for setting classroom performance standards is unparalleled outside of higher education. However, because they value the freedom to do as they please once they enter the classroom, they typically face this responsibility with only token support from their colleagues and the administration. What college teachers have accepted is a massive leadership challenge. Having assumed sole responsibility for guiding students toward academic objectives, they have also accepted the lonely burden of meeting behavioral objectives: promoting civility and dealing with occasional unpleasantness. This can be a heavy and even frightening burden at times, especially since college teachers typically have little more than common sense and goodwill to guide them. Few of them have received training in community building or conflict management. If they are lucky, their classes run smoothly, or at least without difficulties apparent to the outside world. If not, incivility may suddenly become a leadership challenge for a department chair or dean to handle. This shift commonly implies a quantum leap in stress for the teacher and the students, and an unwelcome surprise for the administrator.

This chapter explores ways in which a department chair can work in partnership with teachers to promote or restore civility. I consider two broad questions: What can a chair do to help faculty develop a civil learning environment? and How should a chair assist if incivility is beyond a faculty member's ability to manage? These questions are important because the chair not only shares responsibility for the students' welfare and growing intellectual maturity, but is also charged with professional development of the faculty and the integrity of the academic unit. My underlying thesis is that effective leadership at all levels is a key to promoting civility in academia.

Technical Versus Adaptive Situations

Many of the tasks that we perform each day are routine. We have done them many times before and have established rules by which we can make decisions in a consistent and predictable way. A repertoire of standard solutions reduces the job of problem solving to one of diagnosis and application, reducing stress and uncertainty for everyone. In constructing a syllabus, for example, a teacher may define a grading scale, set up policies for dealing with late assignments and unexcused absences, provide an outline of required readings, and offer a calendar of important deadlines. A student who scores 79 on an exam earns a predictable C+, and one who studies Chapter 2 as assigned is prepared for in-class discussion.

Situations that can be managed in this way have been called *technical situations* (Heifetz, 1994). Provided that we can diagnose them correctly and apply the appropriate rules, we are assured of a specific outcome. The rules may be formalized in a syllabus or a university catalogue, or they may be ad hoc rules that evolve during a class to govern such matters as the order in which people speak during a debate. A teacher may need management skills in technical situations, particularly if the rules are complex, but needs few leadership skills, since the rules limit acceptable options. A significant characteristic of leadership, implicit by its absence in the technical context, is creative decision making in the face of ambiguity.

True leadership becomes necessary in situations that Heifetz has called *adaptive*. These are situations in which a problem to be addressed may be well defined but in which the appropriate solution or the outcome is uncertain, or situations in which it may not even be clear how to define the problem. Predefined rules do not apply unambiguously in adaptive situations. For some adaptive situations, in fact, there may be no rules in advance. Unlike technical situations, adaptive situations require leadership because they force individuals to recognize uncertainty and invent new rules. More important, they obligate individuals to clarify and reconcile competing values as they adapt to unfamiliar circumstances. For example, a teacher may lead the class to decide which is more important for their success: independent learning or collaborative skills? spontaneous questions or polite silence? a well-written paper or a paper completed on time?

A classroom is an adaptive environment. Students are faced continually with unfamiliar observations and ideas and are expected to alter their worldview in consequence. Learning therefore involves risk. Values that we associate with learning beckon students away from the safety they feel in ignorance. Their predictable response is uneasiness or discomfort. A teacher, then, has two leadership tasks. One is the constructive work involved with helping willing students to resolve their discomfort by applying their self-discipline and capable minds to learning. By and large, this is pleasant work of cajoling, teasing, challenging, stretching, and applauding. The less pleasant leadership task is dealing with students who try to resolve discomfort by denying it, retreating to more familiar technical positions instead of adapting. For these students, a teacher's teasing, cajoling, and challenging can lead to hostility or other forms of uncivil behavior. If we add to this latter group students who come to class reluctantly, those who bring unresolved conflicts with them, and those whose typical behavior is uncivil, the teacher's leadership task begins to look frighteningly unattractive.

Administrative Support for Civility

Viewed from this perspective, a department chair's challenge is to model good leadership skills to help teachers learn to become more effective leaders themselves. Most of us do not learn leadership skills effectively without guidance. Rather, we learn by studying what works for effective leaders and modeling their behavior in our own settings. Building on the chair's example, an individual teacher can use the same principles to improve leadership in the classroom. The following suggestions are therefore not only a prescription for leadership by the department chair. They reveal aspects of leadership that apply equally well in the classroom once a teacher has mastered them.

Leadership Builds on Knowledge. A department chair should create faculty development opportunities for teachers under his or her direction. In collaboration with a campus faculty development center, if one is available, the chair can sponsor seminars to hone teaching skills or address difficult classroom situations. Faculty may be encouraged to participate in off-campus workshops or institutes on leadership and college teaching, or to attend programs led by visiting experts. The department chair can make articles related to classroom practice available in a central location or may subscribe to periodicals such as *Teaching Professor* that offer novel perspectives on teaching.

A department chair must be sure that faculty are familiar with their rights and responsibilities as teachers and that they are aware of policies and procedures that support them. University charters, faculty and student handbooks, course catalogues, and office procedure guides outline standard expectations for common classroom situations. These include grading policies, procedures for adding or dropping a class, protocols for dealing with academic dishonesty or with sexual or racial harassment, and statements regarding free speech and intellectual property. Under typical conditions, these define a technical framework in which a well-informed teacher can manage student concerns. Under less certain adaptive circumstances, these basic policies and procedures provide a point of departure for creative problem solving and circumscribe the universe within which ad hoc decisions can be made.

These same basic policies and expectations should be shared with students. A teacher will find the job of maintaining credibility and the respect of students much easier if everyone understands and accepts the rules. In this regard, the teacher's leadership role is that of an adviser.

Leadership Is a Shared Activity. Instead of leaving each faculty member to devise effective teaching strategies and conflict resolution techniques by trial and error, a departmental chair should encourage faculty to work together. If collaboration is unfamiliar to them, faculty will focus on curricular issues initially. Encourage teachers not to stop there, however. A chair should anticipate sources of classroom stress and let faculty draw on their collective experience and insight to pose coping strategies. A department chair, in other words, can develop leadership abilities among teaching faculty, at the same time improving basic pedagogy and promoting civility by urging faculty to learn from each other.

Teachers who learn to share their classroom successes and failures usually discover that these lessons are the foundation for many active learning methods that motivate student learning and improve the student-teacher relationship. However, active learning is not easy for most teachers to manage, in large part because an active classroom is highly adaptive, requiring leadership, while a lecture is more controlled and technical. Teachers may also find that active learning, because it builds on uncertainty, creates more opportunities for overt incivility than a lecture. Anticipating those opportunities, turning them into constructive teachable moments, and diverting stress into learning rather than misbehavior require leadership. By encouraging teachers to develop leadership skills through collaboration with each other and through emulating the chair's own collaborative style, then, the chair improves the pedagogical climate and reduces the likelihood of incivility.

Leadership Means Exploring Choices. Good planning may foster learning and civility and may reduce the likelihood of unexpected behavior in the classroom, but neither outcome is guaranteed. Adaptive environments are inherently risky. Effective leaders must be flexible, willing to consider alternative solutions to any challenge. Teachers, as leaders, must learn to diagnose student behavior quickly and adjust to shifting circumstances. In the simplest situations, a teacher may choose among familiar, preconsidered options, essentially reducing an adaptive situation to a set of technical ones. Most teachers, for example, draw on a standard repertoire of responses when students arrive late to class. Leadership in such cases may mean little more than management by the book, but still it involves weighing the advantages of possible strategies in qualitatively different classroom contexts. In more complex situations, a teacher may need to devise untested solutions to unprecedented challenges.

A department chair can help teachers practice their skills under semicontrolled conditions by regularly involving them in decision making, under the guidance of more experienced colleagues. Team teaching, shared advising, and service on student-faculty liaison or grievance committees can help teachers develop a facility for dealing with new situations while minimizing their personal risk. A teacher learns flexibility through practice, becoming more adept at anticipating and avoiding incivility.

Effective Leadership Is Motivational. Even when teachers are competent and have the capacity for good judgment in leading a classroom, they may lack confidence. To avoid possible unpleasantness, a risk-averse teacher may fail to take action in the face of incivility, thus tacitly reinforcing poor behavior. A department chair can promote leadership by acknowledging the teacher's uneasiness, reinforcing the teacher's positive actions, and recognizing their success. A well-chosen word offered privately can reassure teachers who face uncertain situations. Public acknowledgment that teachers have met difficult challenges can give a department's faculty confidence that they can address even greater challenges in the future. Emulating this aspect of leadership, a teacher should reward the positive actions that a class takes to resolve conflicts and promote civility among its members. Given recognition for dealing with difficult situations in constructive ways, students can become allies in building a respectful classroom community.

Effective Leadership Emphasizes Values. Underlying each of the preceding points is the assumption that an effective leader shapes the environment in which choices are made and provides tools for decision making, generally guiding others in resolving adaptive challenges. In the student-centered language that has become common, we often hear that a teacher should be a "guide on the side," not a "sage on the stage." In these words, we see another aspect of leadership: although prepared to make decisions alone if necessary, an effective leader prefers to develop the community's ability to make its own decisions.

Edward Hallowell (1997) has reminded us that "students will connect with each other, as they always have. But they need the elder presence, now perhaps more than ever, because so many students have grown up with so little guidance from home. Professors don't have to be parents to college students, but they can be their intellectual fathers and mothers, shapers and sharpeners of their minds." To this, we should add that teachers have a responsibility for helping students clarify the values that shape conduct both inside and outside the classroom. As a leader, a teacher cannot be value neutral. Without being dogmatic or blindly proscriptive, a teacher can lead students in the habits of civility by sharing his or her values openly and modeling behavior consistent with those values. Civil behavior, then, can become the class's decision rather than a decision imposed by the teacher. To encourage this facet of leadership, a department chair faced with the challenge of helping teachers promote civility in the classroom should facilitate discussions among the faculty not merely about their classroom practices but, more fundamentally, about their shared values.

Each group of teachers will phrase values differently and prioritize them differently in the mix. Respect for the efforts of others may be important, for example, or pride in a task that is well done and completed on time. Conciseness, clarity of expression, originality, and persistence may also be reflected in what teachers say they value. These form unspoken assumptions that shape our own behavior in the classroom, and yet too often, they remain unspoken and are lost on students. By helping faculty to articulate the values that underlie their teaching, a department chair can help them discover a focus for classroom leadership and a basis for civil interaction with students.

Administrative Leadership When Things Go Wrong

Despite good planning and all efforts to cultivate civility, teachers still face the academic version of Murphy's Law: uncertainty is the only predictable characteristic of classroom behavior. Misunderstandings occur, lack of sleep leads to frayed nerves, the teacher loses a graded assignment, a disagreement between roommates spills over into the classroom, a student peeks at a neighbor's exam in a moment of weakness, or the basketball team decides to practice three-point shots from the back row. If the department chair has stressed leadership development among teaching faculty, most of these events can be managed adroitly in the classroom. What about those few occasions—we can always hope that they are few—when the teacher cannot deal with the incivility, and it becomes the department chair's problem?

By the time incivility demands the chair's attention, it may well have escalated too far to resolve easily. It has landed in the chair's office precisely because it is too knotty for the teacher to handle or, if it is a student bringing the complaint, because the teacher is perceived to be the root of the problem. Furthermore, the situation may have worsened while the teacher, reluctant to admit failure, has tried a series of fruitless remedies or after the student, afraid of reprisals, has suffered repeated injustices. The chair may hear of the difficulty for the first time, in fact, after it has already become a serious problem. For all parties to a classroom conflict, the involvement of an administrator can signal heightened tension, the hardening of positions, and a tendency to fix blame rather than to seek resolution. The chair's immediate task, then, is to clarify his or her own role as a leader—a role that will vary depending on how open the conflict is.

Negotiated Resolution.   Most cases that come to a chair involve an open disagreement between a teacher and one or more students. A student may feel unfairly penalized for repeated absences, for example, or a teacher may have a chronic problem with students who sabotage others' group assignments. All parties are aware that a problem exists, although they may disagree strongly about the nature of the problem and how it should be handled.

In all but the most trivial cases, a solution imposed by the chair will be less satisfying than one that the teacher and students negotiate with the chair's help. The chair, then, must be clear that his or her role is to facilitate a resolution, not to mandate one. Initially this announcement may meet with some resistance, because parties to the dispute have already failed to agree and are hoping for the chair to make a decision for them. Both, in fact, commonly assume that the chair will take the teacher's side in deciding what to do. Even when this is likely—or, perhaps, especially when it is likely—it is unwise for the chair to relieve the teacher and students of their responsibility to participate in the resolution.

The first step in negotiating a resolution is to separate the people from the problem as much as possible. By the time a dispute reaches the chair's office, personality issues may have made it difficult to address the problem itself. As tempers mount, parties to a disagreement tend to make ad hominem inferences about each other's motives rather than focusing on the original point of disagreement. In attempts to gain the upper hand in a growing dispute, people typically rely on posturing for each other, simultaneously protecting their own egos and trying to weaken their opponents' egos. The chair's first goal should be to convince the parties to work together to solve the problem that they share, leaving aside their feelings about each other.

The job of separating people from the problem is complicated in an academic setting because of the uneven power relationships between teachers and students. French and Raven (1960) describe five types of power relationships, all of which can be found in a classroom:

1. Reward power, based on a student's perception that the teacher can dispense rewards (such as grades or recommendations) for performance or behavior
2. Coercive power, based on a student's perception that the teacher can punish poor performance or behavior
3. Legitimate power, based on a student's perception that the teacher's status or title authorizes the teacher to make and enforce rules
4. Expert power, based on a student's perception that the teacher has special knowledge and experience
5. Referent power, based on the student's desire to emulate the teacher and thus share the teacher's power

In general, these relationships are tilted in favor of the teacher. Teachers and students know this. When the department chair joins a negotiation, however, the relationships change because both the teacher and the students perceive the chair's greater legitimate power. Paradoxically, then, intervention by the chair increases the perceived seriousness of the dispute but at the same time gives the students and teacher a chance to shift their focus away from power and personalities.

Too often a disagreement becomes framed by statements that reflect each party's fears and desires about the other party's behavior instead of expressing their own underlying interests. A department chair, acting as a disinterested party, can reduce the emotional tension between a teacher and student by asking each to restate the problem briefly without making interpretive statements. In doing this, the chair is beginning to redirect their attention to interests rather than positions. Neither person's restatement may seem reasonable to the other person, but each has taken an important step by focusing on his or her own interests rather than the other's behavior (see Chapter Five, this volume).

The chair's next goal in negotiation should be to lead the teacher and student toward finding options for mutual gain instead of staying on opposite sides of an argument. A teacher and student might consider ways to make the final minutes of the class period more interesting and intellectually rewarding, for example. The idea in this process is not to strive at first for a unique solution, but to brainstorm possible alternatives that may meet the interests that each person has expressed. The chair should resist generating alternatives if possible, placing that responsibility on the teacher and student. This forces them to remain engaged in the process of dispute resolution and increases the chance that the end result will be one that they can both live with. It will be more difficult later for the disputants to abandon a solution that they have created than it would be to walk away from a solution that the chair had imposed on them.

Once the teacher and student have agreed that a particular solution best satisfies their interests, the final task is to determine objective standards for future performance. It should not be enough to agree that "we need to improve communication between the students and the teacher" or "the teacher ought to return graded papers more quickly." Negotiated agreements without specific performance expectations are easy to ignore. Instead the chair should insist, for example, that the teacher make a practice of arriving at least five minutes early for class or that students be expected to show up during office hours at least once a month. If a teacher has accused a student of plagiarism, both parties may agree to have the student's work reviewed by a third person or a panel of students and faculty. This sort of agreement creates benchmarks against which to measure progress and compliance, as well as a deterrent against further disagreeable activity.

The process outlined here is described in much greater detail by Fisher and Ury (1991) and Ury (1991) as *principled negotiation*. As with the constructive leadership principles already discussed in this chapter, it is a process that can be used not only by the department chair but also by a teacher who must negotiate disputes between students.

Issues Involving Confidentiality. Perhaps the most difficult problems that reach the chair's office are those that involve a request for confidentiality. Allegations of sexual harassment or personal discrimination are examples, as are many situations of academic dishonesty. The chair typically has the first hint of conflict when a nervous student appears at the office door and says, "I have a terrible problem with my teacher, and I need to talk about it. Could we close the door?" or when a teacher says, "I think a student in my class has been cheating, but he's a big guy and I'm afraid to confront him." In these settings, the chair's leadership role is that of a counselor rather than a facilitator.

Aside from the challenge that the problem itself presents, the chair must balance the interests of all parties for both confidentiality and fairness, as well as the institution's integrity. Before hearing the complaint, the chair should take care to tell the complainant that there may be circumstances under which he or she would not be able to maintain confidentiality—for example, conditions in which the rights of others might be compromised, or more drastic situations when a court may order disclosure. If appropriate, the chair should suggest instead a private meeting between the complainant and a physician, a licensed counselor, or a member of the clergy who has a legal responsibility for respecting confidentiality. Finally, because concerns about confidentiality are commonly coupled with fears about reprisal, the chair must make a firm and clear statement that any attempts at retaliation will be dealt with decisively.

Confidential meetings are one-sided, so the chair will be hearing only one party's interpretation of an alleged incivility. It may be difficult to separate personal issues from the facts of the situation, so the chair should avoid committing to a specific course of action beyond making a sincere promise to investigate further. If the chair's ability to follow through on that promise will be severely limited by the request for confidentiality, then he or she should make it clear that no action can be taken. This can be a highly frustrating conclusion, especially if the chair feels some sympathy for the person who has revealed an apparent injustice, but to act without hearing both sides of an alleged problem would be unethical and could create an even greater injustice.

Depending on the nature of the problem, the chair may be obligated by law or by university policy to contact a student conduct officer, the affirmative action office, the office of legal counsel, the campus security office, or some other body even if he or she has only heard one side of the alleged problem. The chair should also weigh the severity of the problem and its implications for the integrity of the institution and decide whether to inform the dean or some other senior administrator. This is a particularly wise step if the problem has legal, financial, or personnel implications that may eventually extend beyond the department.

In short, although parties in an academic dispute may share confidential information with the chair, it is rarely a good idea to use that information as the basis for resolving the dispute. If all information is offered confidentially, no resolution is possible. Unless the problem can be brought to a negotiated settlement or transferred to the authority of a body that can make an adjudicated decision (such as a student conduct committee), the chair can do little more than hear the private information, offer counsel, and hope that the problem will not worsen.

Leadership in a Crisis. A chair's worst nightmare is violent, uncontrolled incivility. Fortunately, threats to personal safety and damage to property are rare in colleges, although celebrated incidents send ripples of concern across campuses from time to time. Burroughs (1990) and Kearney and Plax (1992) report a typology of nineteen different types of resistance techniques, from which students are least likely to favor "active resistance," "disruption," and "challenging the teacher's basis of power." Their findings suggest that college students would rather avoid open and aggressive confrontations with their teachers because passive resistance strategies generally work better for them and because students are conditioned socially to passive classroom roles. Nevertheless, as Kuhlenschmidt and Layne note in Chapter Five in this volume, substance abuse and some forms of mental illness can lead to unpredictable behavior among students and, occasionally, among teachers.

Few department chairs are trained in crisis intervention. As a result, the appropriate action in almost all cases is immediate notification of trained people in campus security, the medical center, or student counseling services. The chair's leadership responsibility, once professionals have been notified, is to work with the teacher to ensure the stability of the class.

Conclusion

In the interest of promoting civility, a department chair's task is to build a strong, trusting relationship with teaching faculty and, through them, with students. When that relationship is strained by incivility, the chair's task is to provide counsel and to negotiate resolutions and new relationships. Both responsibilities call for leadership. The skills of leadership correspond very closely with good teaching skills. The importance of open communication, collaborative problem solving, recognition of accomplishments, and the deliberate discussion of values cannot be underscored too heavily. Neither can the importance of cultivating the skills of principled negotiation and confidential listening. In a sense, then, the department chair's challenge to promote civility is simply a facet of his or her larger challenge to assure students that they will have talented and supportive teachers. The departmental chair, as leader, is teaching the faculty how to become more effective leaders in their classrooms.

References

Burroughs, N. F. "The Relationship of Teacher Immediacy and Student Compliance—Resistance with Learning." Unpublished doctoral dissertation, West Virginia University, 1990.
Fisher, R., and Ury, W. *Getting to Yes: Negotiating Agreement Without Giving In.* (2nd ed.) New York: Penguin, 1991.
French, J.R.P., Jr., and Raven, B. "The Bases of Social Power." In D. Cartwright and A. Zander (eds.), *Group Dynamics.* New York: HarperCollins, 1960.
Hallowell, E. M. "I Am Here Because They Were There." *About Campus,* 1997, 2 (4), 16–22.
Heifetz, R. *Leadership Without Easy Answers.* Cambridge, Mass.: Harvard University Press, 1994.
Kearney, P., and Plax, T. G. "Student Resistance to Control." In V. P. Richmond and J. C. McCroskey (eds.), *Power in the Classroom: Communication, Control, and Concern.* Hillsdale N.J.: Erlbaum, 1992.
Ury, W. *Getting Past No: Negotiating with Difficult People.* New York: Bantam, 1991.

STEVEN M. RICHARDSON *is vice provost for undergraduate affairs and dean of undergraduate studies at Bowling Green State University.*

As we observe the world around us, it is increasingly obvious that we must be the guardians of our own civility. Here we discuss some theories and devise some ways to institutionalize civility and to resolve problems when it breaks down.

The Prevention and Cure of Campus Disputes

Richard Hebein

> It is the witnessing of your talent at achieving such a result that makes me judge you an excellent go-between. For the man who can recognize those who are fitted to be mutually helpful and can make them desire one another's acquaintance, that man, in my opinion, could also create friendship between cities and arrange suitable marriages, and would be a very valuable acquisition as friend or ally for both states and individuals.
> —Xenophon, *Symposium* (c. 380 B.C.)

Enough has been said about the problem; we seem to be becoming an increasingly uncivil society, and campus reflects the larger society. Although we cannot cure society's ills, behavior on campuses today will affect the behavior of the next generation in the larger society. And behavior on campus is comparatively easy to shape through consciousness raising, communication, interaction, and the articulation of campus values. The other chapters in this volume have stressed interpersonal relationships and the importance of awareness, communication and interaction in the creation of tolerance, trust, respect, and civility in the classroom. Let us turn our attention now to the campus atmosphere.

Promoting an Institutional Atmosphere

Civility thrives in the classroom to the extent that it is embraced by the campus community at large. A teacher, or even a department, cannot promote civility alone. Direction from the top is essential for setting a campus climate.

If the administration says nothing, that in itself sets a tone for the campus. Our mothers told us that actions speak louder than words, but the words are important too.

College presidents have always enjoyed the privilege of shaping the way campus communities see themselves. Robert Maynard Hutchins, president of the University of Chicago in the middle years of this century, spoke forcefully about the need for a "vision of the end," without which he could see nothing but "aimlessness" and "vast chaos of the American university" (Hutchins, 1956). From A. Lawrence Lowell and Charles Van Hise to Clark Kerr and beyond, the twentieth century has seen a cavalcade of visionary presidents, or at least those who have tried to steer their campuses through the fog. In recent years, an increasing number have attempted to articulate campus values and behavioral norms. When Sidney A. Ribeau became president at my own campus in 1995, he promulgated a vision and values statement for the University:

> Bowling Green State University aspires to be the premier Learning Community in Ohio, and one of the best in the Nation. Through the interdependence of teaching, learning, scholarship, and service we will create an academic environment grounded in intellectual discovery and guided by rational discourse and civility. Bowling Green State University serves the diverse and multi-cultural communities of Ohio, the United States and the world. The Core Values to which the University adheres are: 1. respect for one another; 2. cooperation; 3. intellectual and spiritual growth; 4. creative imaginings; and 5. pride in a job well done.

This statement is found around the campus and appears in many of the basic publications. More than a mission statement, it sets an official tone for campus behavior. The president refers to it in many of his speeches and talks with various groups. And one can also expect him to say, "And each and every one of you is critically important to our enterprise." Like violence-free zones and honor codes, also increasingly common on college campuses, presidential vision statements become part of the culture.

Forms of Conflict Resolution and Alternative Dispute Resolution

Violence has a long history for settling disputes. It is still much with us, and yet so are more peaceful methods. The establishment of a court system to adjudicate disputes was a major advance in Western civilization. The ancient Greeks were very proud of their court system, and discussion of it permeates their literature. In Aeschylus's trilogy, the *Oresteia,* the goddess Athena comes down to the supreme court to establish its place in Athenian life and to bless its decisions. Sophocles' *Antigone* establishes the importance of the rule of law and the price that the state can exact from people who break it, even when the law is unjust and when people believe that they have justification for breaking it. Its beautiful second chorus ends, "Let the anarchic human be far from my hearth and my home." In transition from the exclusive rule of the sword, the Greeks became a litigious society, a charge often leveled against our own.

Although an improvement over violence, litigation is expensive, and not just in terms of money. Sometimes referred to as a win-lose situation, it leaves a winner who will be happy to some degree and a loser who certainly is not. While this might be an acceptable side effect in a large society where the parties will likely never see each other again, our campuses are too small for litigation to be a satisfactory process. Most disputes occur among people who already know each other and might have to live near and work with each other after the decision. Although direct effects are hard to calculate, disgruntled students and employees arguably contribute to a general lack of respect for and identity with the institution and ultimately to vandalism and other campus crimes.

The high costs of litigation have prompted people to explore other forms of dispute resolution. Grouped together, arbitration, mediation, and conciliation with a number of variations and combinations are known as alternative dispute resolution (ADR) methods. Each is found on college campuses today.

Arbitration. In arbitration, a person who functions very much as a judge usually makes a decision that will be binding on at least one of the parties to a dispute. The decisions are regularly written down, and sometimes the parties are required to accept or reject the decision in writing. Arbitration has been used effectively in settling coal miners' strikes and baseball players' salary disputes. Some college campuses incorporate arbitration into formal procedures for settling grievances among employees.

As one example, the Better Business Bureau (BBB) got into the arbitration business with its Auto Line Program. A trained volunteer arbitrator who works pro bono holds a hearing with a grieving consumer and a representative of the automobile manufacturer at a BBB office. Mechanics can be called in as neutral experts. If the arbitrator determines that a manufacturing defect was the root of the consumer's complaint, he or she can order the manufacturer to make repairs or even to buy the car back. In some states, the BBB is the official agency for hearing complaints under that state's lemon laws.

An intriguing feature of the BBB's Auto Line Program is that the manufacturer agrees in advance to be bound by the decision of the arbitrator, whereas the consumer can either accept or reject the arbitrator's decision and go to court. Why, you might ask, would the manufacturer put itself in a position where it is bound and the consumer is not? The reason is that the manufacturers have found that it is cheaper to use this form of arbitration than litigation. And, in fact, the courts have rarely, if ever, overturned the decision of a BBB arbitrator.

Mediation. In contrast to arbitration, mediation requires the parties in a dispute to reach a resolution themselves. Again there are variations, but the process usually involves bringing the parties into a room with a trained mediator or mediating team. The mediation format is usually structured and follows strict, mutually acceptable ground rules, with the mediator directing the discussion back and forth between the parties. They talk it out until they reach a solution. Most mediators try to reach a resolution in one meeting, but the mediation may extend to multiple sessions. Bringing the parties together face to face can be tense at the outset, but it can be helpful for them to see each other as human beings and to consider their shared desire for an end to conflict.

Peer mediation has worked well in schools and in residence halls for settling disagreements between people from the same sector of the community. The fact that the mediator—a fellow student or fellow employee—might be known to the parties can be an advantage if the mediator has acquired a reputation for impartiality and effectiveness. Furthermore, a peer mediator understands the setting and can succeed, in part, because many people reach agreements more readily in the absence of authority figures.

Conciliation. Conciliation is the least formal method of ADR. In this process, an impartial negotiator (a conciliator) goes back and forth between the parties, trying to arrange a compromise. The phrase *shuttle diplomacy* is apt. Sometimes it is useful to keep the parties away from each other, at least at the beginning of the process. Although sometimes the parties do meet together, the whole process can be completed without such a meeting. A mediation process usually results in a written agreement; conciliations sometimes do not. The result of a conciliation might well be a verbal agreement that the conciliator advises an administrator to take a certain course of action. This type of conclusion is common in corporate and academic institutions where the conciliator might be an ombudsperson who has no authority in the administrative structure and who must identify the appropriate person to implement the agreement that the parties have come to.

The "ombuds" concept arrived on campus in the 1960s. The idea derives from early nineteenth-century Sweden, where the king appointed an ombudsman (literally, a "representative" or "agent") to be an advocate on behalf of citizens in their dealings with the government. Originally ombudspersons were advocates, and they still function this way in some states and municipalities. This type of ombudsperson is called a classical ombudsperson. In contrast, the University and College Ombuds Association's Statement of Ethical Principles requires that campus ombudspersons be neutral, and most campus ombuds offices follow this model. Close to two hundred colleges and universities in North America have ombudspersons who serve the whole campus or its major constituent groups, and an even larger number of ombudspersons serve at the department level. Ombudspersons are more common on large campuses than on small ones, suggesting that more complex communities have more disputes and need more mechanisms to resolve them.

Campus ombudspersons regularly use conciliation to resolve disputes. Some are trained as mediators and use mediation techniques effectively to settle grade disputes and other common academic grievances. There may also be advocacy offices staffed with classical ombudspersons for women and for various minority groups on the same campuses where neutral ombudspersons, mediators, or other types of conciliators work.

ADR clearly comes in many different forms and may be practiced by people who fill a variety of roles on campus. Elements that ADR has in common with adversarial proceedings are familiar to all of us, whether we encounter them in a courtroom, on the battlefield, or in a back alley. I win. You lose. But elements of ADR that are not adversarial are not so instinctively understood. "Fight or flight" is basic to our nature, but ADR requires collaboration, often against our instincts. It is worthy of a "civilized" society.

Conciliation Theory

Before delving into campus structures for resolving disputes, we need to take a detour into conciliation theory, a conceptual framework that underlies all forms of ADR.

A basic tenet of conciliation theory is neutrality. A conciliator, mediator, or arbitrator is effective in dispute resolution because he or she has no personal stake in the outcome and can therefore guide the process without prejudice. That he or she must not take sides cannot be overly emphasized. If the conciliator is leaning toward one side, the other side will sense that, and the effectiveness of the conciliator will be compromised. The neutrality of the conciliator is within his or her control, although the disputing parties frequently try to convince the conciliator that their side is "right." The conciliator may outline what others are likely to see as the strengths and weaknesses of the positions, in order to "objectify" the dispute, but loses effectiveness if he or she becomes identified with the positions themselves.

The second crucial element of conciliation theory is willingness to compromise. When disputants have hardened their positions and have focused on winning, it may be difficult to draw them toward reaching a mutually acceptable solution. They will say that they want to but then drift away from compromise, as evidenced by their actions. Until they recognize a common interest in solving the problem before them, each party identifies solutions that satisfy him or her alone. This leaves underlying issues unresolved or creates ill feelings that resurface in fresh conflict later. It is the conciliator's job to draw the parties back toward compromise. The willingness to compromise is within the control of the parties, but may run counter to their instincts and past experience unless they have the conciliator's guidance.

Conciliation theory postulates that if neutrality and a willingness to compromise are in place, a solution will emerge. This sounds simplistic, but I have watched it work many times. In fact, the solution is usually suggested by one of the parties. After all, they know the dispute better than the conciliator. Frequently the acceptable solution is one that one of the parties suggested early on, but the other party was not in a mood to agree to anything. Unlike litigation and arbitration, conciliation and mediation do not rely on the wisdom of the conciliator or mediator. A judge dispensing the wisdom of Solomon is simply not the way it works. A conciliator is a facilitator.

This is how conciliation works, and it works this way in backyards great and small, and yet ADR is rarely a straightforward task. Whether in the trouble spots of the world or in a domestic setting, when the conflict continues beyond a reasonable time to resolve it, the parties do not have the willingness to compromise. We have to remember that there are individuals who enjoy the conflict more than the resolution. Once the problem is gone, the game is over. Worse than that, as we observe conflict between a minority group and the dominant culture, a disputant's reluctance to compromise may have deep roots in shared societal beliefs and behaviors. Admitting responsibility for wrongdoing or making restitution for a particular action goes way beyond that action and reaches into a disputant's belief system. Because of their beliefs, people feel justified or even compelled to harass members of a minority group, making it difficult for a conciliator to foster a willingness to compromise. Where parties are polarized by group prejudice, it may also be difficult for the conciliator to maintain neutrality.

We have examined arbitration, mediation, and conciliation as theoretical types of ADR and have now considered conciliation theory and some of the practical difficulties in applying it. Let us try to bring this all together so we can then discuss practical structures for dispute resolution on campuses. Arbitration, especially binding arbitration, is quite adversarial. Of the three forms of ADR, this is the one in which the facilitator may face the greatest challenges in applying conciliation theory. A skillful arbitrator can do several things to minimize any lingering hard feelings. He or she can try to get the parties to see the case from the opponent's point of view. During discussions, the arbitrator can explain how he or she sees the case. Hinging the decision on a matter of fact or rule rather than on the motives of the parties will depersonalize the situation. Simply fostering dialogue between the parties can build a bit of trust. These are typical conciliation techniques. It is not necessary, however, for one or even both of the parties to an arbitration to assent to the decision. In this way, conciliation theory is useful but is not a mandatory element of arbitration.

By contrast, mediators and conciliators use conciliation theory extensively. Ideally both parties assent to the decision. In fact, they frequently work toward it as a group. Solutions of this type are characterized as win-win. Because mediators and conciliators take the basic principles of conciliation theory seriously, it is not uncommon for the final result of a resolution to be very different from one that an arbitrator might have declared. Emphasis on compromise and on the neutral role of the facilitator forces disputants to generate their own creative solutions. Only if the emerging solution were patently unfair to one of the parties would the conciliator try to block it.

Neutrality, Advocacy, Confidentiality, and Credibility

A major advantage of ADR over adversarial proceedings is that, in addition to resolving the dispute, both parties can buy into the solution. This is especially important when the parties are members of the same community or when the dispute is one of a persistent series. Endemic tensions between minority groups and the dominant culture frequently manifest themselves in this way. In corporations, minimizing vandalism is an important goal, and losers to a dispute are thought to be prone to vandalism, not only to the other party but to the corporation itself as they try to get even or take out their frustrations. In this way, the institution has an interest in being sure that the parties are satisfied with the resolution of their disputes.

Since we are discussing disputes that occur within a campus community rather than within the larger society where the parties can walk away from each other and from the structure that rendered the decision, the long-term credibility of the dispute resolvers and their processes become extremely important. An ombuds office or mediation center on a college campus is under continuous scrutiny not only by current clients but also by potential future ones. Even more than in the public sector, the credibility of a dispute resolver (mediator, conciliator, or ombudsperson) rests on two things: neutrality and confidentiality.

In discussing conciliation theory, we emphasized the importance of neutrality to effective mediation and conciliation outcomes. It is also important to consider how neutrality affects the continued credibility of a campus mediator or conciliator. Possibly because some ombudspersons in the public arena still assume the classical role of an advocate, clients of campus ADR services are often confused about the importance of neutrality. The conciliator does not "take sides"; the advocate does. Conciliators never determine who is right; an advocate presumes that the client is. Both roles can be important in a community. For example, some hospitals have both patient ombudspersons and patient advocates. The ombudsperson and the advocate can each approach the hospital administrator in connection with the same patient. Both can work to resolve that patient's problem, but the interpersonal dynamics will be different. Similarly, a campus ombuds office and various offices such as a Latino students' organization, a faculty senate, and a staff union can all serve a college or university community. Conciliators and advocates in these can be equally effective; everybody just needs to know where they stand.

Confidentiality is the other foot on which credibility rests, and much can be said about it too, but the following should suffice for our purposes. Several ombudspersons have shown their willingness to go to jail for contempt of court for failing to divulge information and breach confidentiality because one public breach will destroy the credibility of the ombudsperson and the office. The fact that courts may impose penalties on the institution for each day that the ombudsperson fails to comply makes this a very difficult matter that needs resolution itself. Although ombudspersons who work for the states (five states have ombudspersons) have their rights to confidentiality delineated by law, campus ombudspersons have no such protection. Campus ombuds organizations are working for shield laws, but given the larger movement for disclosure, legislatures are reluctant to grant such protection; protection of confidentiality is being granted by some courts in individual cases. Campus ombudspersons frequently explain to their clients that the confidentiality of their records is not protected by law but that they will make every effort to uphold confidentiality to the extent that they can. As a result campus ombudspersons typically keep only minimal records or notes. The fact that ombudspersons have risked contempt of court illustrates the importance of confidentiality in their minds, and the clients rightfully expect as much.

Dispute Resolution Structures

The idea that a college admits and expels its members is at least as old as ancient Rome, where various colleges of priests were organized to maintain the cults and their temples. The processes for making these decisions were, and continue to be, the basis for formal governance and grievance structures. Beginning with the rise of universities in the Middle Ages, college faculty determined who among their ranks would be admitted, promoted, or expelled. The American Association of University Professors still advocates a significant role for faculty in these decisions. Similarly, students have long been under the jurisdiction of deans of students and student courts. As in resolving faculty issues, the presence of peer representatives in these processes is thought to yield more credible results. Finally, whether organized into collective bargaining units or not, various employee groups gained the right to file grievances, frequently with significant peer input. The operative principle for each major constituent group on campus is that people should be judged by their peers.

Campus grievance procedures typically allow the grievant to claim relief for alleged wrongdoing on the part of someone else. The matter is considered by a panel composed at least in part of peers, and a recommendation including a remedy is issued to the student, faculty, or staff member. Although not courts of law with either their force or procedures, the goal of these grievance panels is fundamental fairness. As in courts of law, their processes are adversarial, and they determine winners and losers. These processes are familiar, and we need not go into greater detail here.

Nonadversarial dispute resolution is also an old idea, but we saw a notable resurgence of it in the 1960s on campuses and throughout society generally. On my own campus, a mandatory attempt at conciliation before the hearing became part of the faculty grievance procedure during that era. More recently alternatives to the formal hearing were added: the grievant can choose to have the panel hear the case without the presence of the parties or witnesses, and the panel works only from the documents submitted. Or the grievant can choose to have the dispute submitted to the vice president for academic affairs or a designee for resolution. Again, that person works only from the documents. These alternatives, although still adversarial, are less confrontational.

Several models for campus dispute resolution structures are even less adversarial. They can be unit based, such as a department conciliator for student grades or a residence hall peer mediation team. They can be constituency based, such as a faculty or a student ombudsperson. Student ombudspersons are somewhat common on Canadian campuses. These structures can coexist with campuswide university ombuds services. A campuswide ADR officer will usually let the unit ADR person try to resolve a problem first since problems are best resolved locally.

The great advantage that a campuswide ombudsperson usually has is that he or she typically reports to the campus president. This announces the importance of the function and suggests that the cooperation of all is expected. Although the reporting line is to the president, ombuds offices only rarely communicate with the president about a specific case, and with the permission of the client. Under unusual circumstances, for example, it might be necessary to ask the president to encourage the cooperation of an office in obtaining data or enforcing an agreement. Ombuds offices usually make brief annual reports to the presidents and their communities. Aggregate demographic information is usually included, but all identifiers of individual cases are removed. At that time, any records or notes that might have accumulated throughout the prior year are destroyed except for continuing cases.

There are various ways of staffing an ombuds office or mediation center. One possibility is to hire professional career ombudspersons and mediators. Another is to choose students, faculty, and other employees to serve for a given term. There are places where persons of appropriate temperament can go for training. Temperament and good interpersonal skills are important; the techniques can be learned.

Costs of an ombuds office or mediation center are easy to project; the savings are not. Confidentiality and the nonmonetary nature of many disputes make it difficult to arrive at a figure. However, one has only to contemplate the costs of a wrongful dismissal case to realize that the stakes are high. A conciliation step might have fostered some very helpful dialogue. And the mere existence of an ombuds or similar office on campus says to the community that this is a civilized place where the institution has an interest in the peaceful resolution of the inevitable disputes. Regardless of the structures for ADR, the fact that nonadversarial problem solving is institutionalized on a campus says that this is a cherished value here and that this is a civilized place.

Reference

Hutchins, R. M. *Freedom, Education, and the Fund: Essays and Addresses, 1946–1956.* New York: Meridian, 1956.

RICHARD HEBEIN *is associate dean of arts and sciences and a former campus ombudsman at Bowling Green State University.*

INDEX

Abbott, R. D., 38
Active listening, 7–8
Adams, M., 71
Adaptive situations, 78–79
Administration. *See* Department chair; Leadership
Advocacy, with alternative dispute resolution (ADR), 93
Aeschylus, 88
Affect checking, 8
Aggression, redirected, as cause of behavior problems, 52
Alberti, R., 55
Allen, A., 38, 40
Alternative dispute resolution (ADR), 89–91; characteristics of, 92–94; methods for, 89–91; structures for, 94–95; theory underlying, 91–92. *See also* Conflict management
American Association of University Professors, 94
American Psychiatric Association, 51
Anderson, J. A., 70, 71
Angelo, T. A., 39, 49
Antigone (Sophocles), 88–89
Arbitration, 9, 89, 92
Assigned seats, in large classes, 40, 53
Assumptions: effect of, on teaching/learning, 18–21; examining, 22; of students, 18–19; underlying emotions, 17–18
Attention seeking, as cause of behavior problems, 52
Ayers, W., 33

Bainer, D. L., 71
Baseball caps, classroom wearing of, 59–60
Behavior problems: changing behaviors contributing to, 54–56; ignoring, 37–38; instructor rapport and, 71; in large classes, 35–43; mediation of, 73; organizational activities for dealing with, 74–75; questions for analyzing, 46–49; reasons for, 49–54; requiring professional intervention, 48; strategies for dealing with, 45–56; training in dealing with, 74. *See also* Conflicts; Incivility
Beliefs. *See* Assumptions

Better Business Bureau (BBB), 89
Billson, J. M., 5, 69, 72
Bishop, M., 59
Bowling Green State University, vision statement of, 88
Boyer Commission on Educating Undergraduates in the Research University, 27
Brainstorming, 9, 65
Broken Cord, The (Dorris), 42
Brooke, C. P., 10
Brookfield, S. D., 26
Brown, T. J., 71
Burroughs, N. F., 85

Cameron, P. M., 5
Carbone, E., 28, 36
Catastrophe theory, 3; applied to teacher-learner alliance, 10–11
Cheating, in large classes, 42–43
Chemical imbalance, dealing with emotions caused by, 21
Clark, L., 16
Classroom: as adaptive environment, 78–79; establishing climate for diversity in, 72–73; sense of security in, 11, 69
Communication: about sensitive issues, 28–30; of expectations for behavior, 36–37, 49, 52, 59–60; immediacy of, 70; incivility as form of, 3–4
Compromise, willingness to, 91
Conciliation, 90, 92
Conciliation theory, 91–92
Confidentiality: of alternative dispute resolution (ADR), 93–94; with e-mail, 29; leadership with issues involving, 84–85
Conflict management, 60, 61–67; problem identification in, 61–64; solution identification in, 64–66; solution implementation in, 66–67. *See also* Alternative dispute resolution (ADR)
Conflicts, 59; as strengthening relationship, 5; in teacher-learner alliance, 5–6; training in dealing with, 74. *See also* Behavior problems; Incivility
Contracts, educational, 9
Control, perception of, 19–21
Counseling, 9, 10, 30, 48
Cowley, W. H., 59

97

Back Issue/Subscription Order Form

Copy or detach and send to:
Jossey-Bass Inc., Publishers, 350 Sansome Street, San Francisco CA 94104-1342

Call or fax toll free!
Phone 888-378-2537 6AM-5PM PST; Fax 800-605-2665

Back issues: Please send me the following issues at $23 each
(Important: please include series initials and issue number, such as TL90)

1. TL _____

_____

_____

$ _____   Total for single issues

$ _____   Shipping charges (for single issues *only;* subscriptions are exempt from shipping charges): Up to $30, add $5^{50} • $30^{01}–$50, add $6^{50} $50^{01}–$75, add $7^{50} • $75^{01}–$100, add $9 • $100^{01}–$150, add $10 Over $150, call for shipping charge

Subscriptions   Please ❏ start   ❏ renew my subscription to *New Directions for Teaching and Learning* for the year 19___ at the following rate:

❏ Individual $56   ❏ Institutional $99
NOTE: Subscriptions are quarterly, and are for the calendar year only. Subscriptions begin with the spring issue of the year indicated above. For shipping outside the U.S., please add $25.

$ _____   Total single issues and subscriptions (CA, IN, NJ, NY and DC residents, add sales tax for single issues. NY and DC residents must include shipping charges when calculating sales tax. NY and Canadian residents only, add sales tax for subscriptions)

❏ Payment enclosed (U.S. check or money order only)

❏ VISA, MC, AmEx, Discover Card #_____ Exp. date_____

Signature _____ Day phone _____

❏ Bill me (U.S. institutional orders only. Purchase order required.)

Purchase order #_____

Name _____

Address _____

_____

_____

Phone_____ E-mail _____

For more information about Jossey-Bass Publishers, visit our Web site at:
www.josseybass.com   **PRIORITY CODE = ND1**